STUDY SKILLS HAND BOOK

A Guide for All Teachers

Kenneth G. Graham
Seaford, New York, Public Schools

H. Alan Robinson
Hofstra University

 International Reading Association
800 Barksdale Road, Box 8139, Newark, Delaware 19714

 Clearinghouse on Reading and Communication Skills
National Institute of Education

International Reading Association
800 Barksdale Road, Newark, Delaware 19714

Clearinghouse on Reading and Communication Skills
1111 Kenyon Road, Urbana, Illinois 61801

This publication was prepared with funding from the National Institute of Education, U.S. Department of Education, under contract no. 400-83-0025. Contractors undertaking such projects under government sponsorship are encouraged to express freely their judgment in professional and technical matters. Prior to publication, the manuscript was submitted to the Publications Committee of the IRA for critical review and determination of professional competence. This publication has met such standards. Points of view or opinions, however, do not necessarily represent the official view or opinions of either the International Reading Association or the National Institute of Education.

Library of Congress Cataloging in Publication Data

Graham, Kenneth G.
　Study skills handbook: A guide for all teachers.

　Bibliography: p.
　1. Study, Method of.　2. Reading comprehension.
I. Robinson, H. Alan, 1921-　　.II. Title.
LB1049.G72　　1984　　　　371.3′028′1　　　　84-3817
ISBN 0-87207-858-2

Fourth Printing, April 1987

CONTENTS

FOREWORD

Being able to study efficiently and effectively is vital to a student's academic success, especially in today's fast changing world. Despite the importance of study skills, insufficient attention is given in many classrooms to help students to develop proficiency in their use. Study skills are important for elementary, secondary, and college students. Not only are persons who are deficient in study skills handicapped in academic settings, they also are handicapped in many of today's occupations. Many adults enter occupations in which the procedures of operation and technology are constantly changing, thus necessitating regular study of documents such as technical manuals, procedural guides, and directives. Occupational survival often rests upon workers' abilities to study well enough to keep abreast of changes in the occupation itself.

Though teachers of reading give some attention to study skills, much of the direct instruction in techniques of study should come in subject matter areas. The elementary teacher likely would give most attention to the development of these important skills in subject areas such as in geography, science, or history. Secondary teachers also have heavy responsibilities for the continued development of study skills.

Graham and Robinson, in *Study Skills Handbook: A Guide for All Teachers*, offer very practical suggestions for the development of study strategies. Several features of this publication enhance its value considerably for busy elementary or secondary teachers who want to improve their competence in helping students become more effective in studying. Each chapter begins with a study guide and closes with a reaction guide, thus illustrating for the reader an excellent study strategy that teachers may use with text materials in their classes.

In keeping with a characteristic of a good handbook, the authors do not assume that readers of this publication are thoroughly familiar with the study strategies themselves; they describe each strategy as well as offer suggestions for developing that strategy. Their publication merges well these descriptions of the various study strategies and practical suggestions for teaching them to students. With strategies as simple as using an index or table of contents to locate information in a single text to strategies as complex as taking a test, writing a report, or developing a study method, the authors leave no stone unturned, no avenue unexplored. The title is quite appropriate in that the publication lives up to what one expects in a *handbook* and also is a reference for *all* teachers.

Ira E. Aaron, *President*
International Reading Association
1983-1984

PREFACE

The Educational Resources Information Center (ERIC) is a national information system operated by the National Institute of Education (NIE) of the U.S. Department of Education. It provides ready access to descriptions of exemplary programs, research and development efforts, and related information useful in developing effective educational programs.

Through its network of specialized centers or clearinghouses, each of which is responsible for a particular educational area, ERIC acquires, evaluates, abstracts, and indexes current significant information and lists this information in its reference publications.

The ERIC Clearinghouse on Reading and Communication Skills, ERIC/RCS, disseminates educational information related to research, instruction, and professional preparation at all levels and in all institutions. The scope of interest of the Clearinghouse includes relevant research reports, literature reviews, curriculum guides and descriptions, conference papers, project or program reviews, and other print materials related to reading, English, educational journalism, and speech communication.

The ERIC system has already made available much informative data through the ERIC Document Reproduction System. However, if the findings of specific educational research are to be intelligible to teachers and applicable to teaching, considerable amounts of data must be reevaluated, focused, and translated into a different context. Rather than resting at the point of making research reports readily accessible, NIE has directed the clearinghouses to work with professional organizations in developing information analysis papers in specific areas within the scope of the clearinghouses.

ERIC is pleased to cooperate with the International Reading Association in making available *Study Skills Handbook: A Guide for All Teachers.*

Charles Suhor
Director, ERIC/RCS

INTRODUCTION

Reading is a process of readers interacting with authors in an attempt to develop meaning—to extend knowledge. This process is of such great importance to academic success that students spend a large portion of their time in the primary grades learning and developing reading strategies. Although students continue to develop and hone reading strategies in the upper grades, the emphasis shifts from learning to use the process to using it in order to learn the content of the curriculum.

A shift from teacher directed to student directed reading activities is to be expected and encouraged as students mature. This shift in responsibilities places greater demands on the skills students have learned for the independent study of content area reading material. Even greater demands must be met by students leaving secondary school for higher education or business.

Study skills and comprehension strategies learned during elementary school years cannot reasonably be expected to meet the needs of students throughout their entire education. Most teachers would agree that the primary goal of education is to teach students how to learn on their own. Yet some teachers concern themselves almost exclusively with content goals and objectives. The development of mature and independent learners is sometimes given a low priority. Fortunately, teachers don't have to choose between teaching the content of the curriculum or the reading process. Both content and process goals may be achieved simultaneously. In this handbook, we explain how.

This handbook is written for the classroom teacher as well as for the reading specialist. Most of the study skills are suitable for use in grades three through ten. Some of the suggested techniques may be adapted for use in the primary grades and some for use in the upper years of high school and the freshman year in college.

Each chapter is organized to capitalize on some of the major study strategies we recommend and each chapter begins with some type of preorganizer and/or concept guide to help you, the reader, mobilize your prior knowledge for the task at hand. Each chapter also includes a short discussion of questions often asked about the ideas dealt with in the chapter. All chapters conclude with a reaction guide to assist you in synthesizing major points and major implications.

We hope you will find both the content and its organization useful as you guide students toward independence in study tasks.

KGG
HAR

ACKNOWLEDGMENTS

We would like to acknowledge with sincere thanks the assistance and contributions of those who aided in the preparation and publication of this book:
- Karl Koenke, Associate Director, ERIC Clearinghouse on Reading and Communication Skills for his support and patience in this project.
- The IRA Publications Committee for their support.
- Faye Branca and the IRA publications staff for preparing the manuscript for publication.
- Stella Sinicki, Supervisor, Hofstra University Office of Special Secretarial Services, for providing the resources of her office during the preparation of the manuscript.
- Dorothy Trombecky, Senior Executive Secretarial Specialist, Hofstra University Office of Special Secretarial Services for word processing the manuscript, and for her patience and professionalism during several revisions.
- The publishers of reprinted material, for generously granting permission to use the many fine works cited in this book.
- Richard J. Northridge, Jr. for his contribution of original art.
- Michelle, Billy, and Danny for their help and encouragement throughout the preparation of this work.

INTERNATIONAL READING ASSOCIATION

Chapter 1
READERS, READING, AND STUDY SKILLS

Advance Organizer

Our present technological civilization has been built upon an accumulation of knowledge passed from individual to individual, generation to generation, down through the ages. The skills of reading and study have also been communicated from teachers to learners since the dawn of written history. Generations of reading researchers have found that the relationship between teacher and learner can greatly influence the kind and amount of learning which takes place. This relationship depends, to a great extent, upon the ability of the teacher to recognize the nature of the individual learner.

Concept Guide

Each of the following terms is defined in context in Chapter 1. As you read about five factors associated with reading and study, complete each of the statements in this guide with the appropriate term from the word list below. Familiarize yourself with this guide and skim the chapter before you begin reading.

anecdotal log	interest interview
assignment sheets	readiness
attitude	study budget
classroom performances	study schedule
comprehension strategies	study skills
cultural background	teacher observation checklist
general knowledge	vocabulary skills

The following statements are numbered in the order in which they appear in the text. Complete each statement with the appropriate term from the vocabulary word list before or during your skimming of this chapter. Change answers if you change your mind.

1. Small changes in _____ can result in large changes in classroom behavior.
2. One structure for "bringing out" the attitudes of individual students is an _____ _____.
3. Keeping an _____ _____ on students whose attitudes seem to interfere with their learning can prove helpful.
4. Part of the distance between reader and writer can be measured in terms of _____ _____.
5. The level of _____ _____ shared by the group of students in your classroom can be considered the least common denominator upon which to base your instructional program.
6. When setting study goals for your students, don't let test scores alone determine your expectations. Reserve judgment until you have had a chance to observe your students' _____ _____.
7. A _____ _____ _____ can be used to gather information about a student's language processing strategies.
8. A checklist on student's reading should be used to help organize the teacher's observations into three categories:
   I. _____ _____
   II. _____ _____
   III. _____ _____
9. _____ for study tasks includes the ability to complete home study assignments, to schedule and budget time for study, and to marshal other task organization skills.
10. Teachers can help students develop task organization skills by providing them with _____ _____, and by helping them prepare a _____ _____ and _____ _____.

Answers:
1. attitude
2. interest interview
3. anecdotal log
4. cultural background
5. general knowledge
6. classroom performance
7. teacher observation checklist
8. I. comprehension strategies
   II. study skills
   III. vocabulary skills
9. readiness
10. assignment sheets, study schedule, study budget

Graham and Robinson

Questions and Answers

Q. What are study skills?

A. Study skills are specific abilities which students may use alone or in combination to learn the content of the curriculum on their own. These abilities are rooted in the reading process. A set of study skills used to solve a problem (like writing a report, or taking a test) is a *strategy*.

Q. Why should these skills be taught?

A. Learning how to learn on their own is more important to students than anything else we can teach them. Teaching study skills means showing students how to solve their problems—which has more to do with how they are taught than what they are taught. After all, the important differences between teachers have to do with *how* they teach, not *what* they teach.

Q. Who should teach study skills?

A. Teachers in every classroom can provide opportunities for using study skills and strategies. The ultimate goal should be the independent use of such strategies by learners as they attempt to unlock the ideas of authors and produce ideas of their own. Most of the classroom proven skills and strategies described in this handbook are directed toward guiding students to learn on their own.

Q. When should these skills be taught?

A. The principles of effective study can (and should) be built into every lesson. Certainly no separate time period is required. As a classroom teacher or reading specialist, you can utilize the materials you use every day. At times you may want to introduce materials that have been specially constructed to emphasize certain study strategies, but the most potent and relevant learning calls for no special materials. The best materials are those which the student must contend with on a daily basis within a classroom and across the total curriculum.

Q. Where do I begin?

A. Most educational programs hinge upon your ability to help students move from where they are now toward a goal of higher achievement. The first step in the process involves offering each learner a realistic challenge to make a desired change. The success or failure of instruction should be determined on the basis of the learning which has taken place. If you are aware of where your students are "coming from," you will be better able to determine how much growth your students should make.

Important Factors to Consider

Quite naturally, there is a distance between the experience of the learner and that of any given writer. This distance is particularly evident when a student is trying to cope with content area materials. "Distance" is the difference between the learner's experience, language, and knowledge and that of the writer.

The distance between reader and writer, then, may be viewed as the amount and type of new information and ideas confronting the learner about to study a given reading selection. As a teacher, you may guide readers across this distance, and help them enjoy the rewards of success for their efforts. In this section we explore briefly those significant factors which contribute to the distance between reader and writer—attitudes, cultural background, general knowledge, general health, linguistic knowledge and flexibility, and readiness for study tasks.

Attitudes

Small changes in attitude can result in large changes in behavior. Attitudes are shaped and influenced by many factors both in and out of school. How students view their educational experiences will depend, to a great extent, upon your attitude as their teacher. You need to become familiar with their attitudes toward many things, but they must also become familiar with your attitudes. Part of helping students close the distance between reader and author is for students to be letter clear about the demands you and the author are making. The students' attitudes should be a serious consideration as the learning task is planned and executed. Those attitudes can be shaped; they need not be static or initiated solely by students.

Show your students that you have a firm view of your role as their teacher, and don't leave them "in the dark" as to their roles and responsibilities as students in your classroom. It is up to you to establish the common ground through which effective communication may take place. The kind of learning which takes place in your classroom will

Graham and Robinson

depend upon the learning environment established with your students. Mutual respect and understanding will provide the kind of rapport you need in order to get down to the business of putting study strategies to use profitably.

Interest interviews. Asking your students about their interests is a way of getting at attitudes and learning more about your students. Getting students to "open up" about themselves individually can provide a great deal of information to the insightful teacher. An interest interview can provide a structure for "bringing out" an individual student. The setting for the interview should be a time when the student won't feel rushed, and it should be a place out of earshot of others. Use the interest interview to "break the ice" and help establish effective communication with your students. (The answers below were given by Paul H., a seventh grader receiving extra help in reading.)

Interest Interview

1. Do you have any hobbies? _____ *hockey, baseball, and*
   _____ *swim team* _____

2. If you were allowed to do whatever you wanted, what would you do? _____ *stay out until 11:00 playing hockey at the*
   _____ *park* _____

3. What television programs do you enjoy? _____ *just* _____
   _____ *baseball and hockey—no particular shows* _____

4. What is the title of the best book you ever read?
   _____ *The Hobbitt by Tolkein* _____

5. Where would you rather be right now? _____ *Quebec—*
   _____ *watching the hockey playoffs* _____

6. Do you read newspapers or magazines? _____ *Sports*
   _____ *Illustrated, Newsweek, and The Daily News Sports*
   _____ *and Comics* _____

7. Do you have a library card? _____ *yes—for any library in*
   _____ *the county* _____

8. What do you do for fun? _____*play hockey and* ATARI_____
   _____*computer games*_____

9. What do you want to be when you grow up?_____*a hockey*_
   _____*player*_____

10. How do you feel about reading? _____*like to read sports*_
    _____*stories and stories about how people overcome*_____
    _____*tragedies, like The Other Side of the Mountain*_____

Insight: Paul is a very personable and well-spoken seventh grade boy. He is bright, yet his report card grades are consistently below average. Paul's height and weight are about average for his age, and he suffers no obvious handicapping conditions. Paul gets along well with others in the classroom setting, and is well liked by his peers. He seems to be quite interested in sports, as are many of his friends. Paul has shown compassion for classmates with problems, and has initiated "team-work" solutions to help them.

Anecdotal logs. Keeping an anecdotal log on students whose attitudes seem to interfere with their learning can prove helpful. Note each specific incident and the measures you have taken. Make it clear to the student when a problem exists, and that it is your desire to help find a solution to the problem. Involve the learner's parents as soon as difficulties develop, and log your observations after each parent contact. Review the student's school records for any information which may help you to understand the attitudes behind the behavior you observe. Reserve judgments until you have apprised yourself of the circumstances which have shaped the behavior you observe.

A form such as the following may prove helpful:

Name of Student _____Donna_____ Grade _____8_____

Address _____

Telephone _____Parent or Guardian _____

Graham and Robinson

Day	Date	Time	Incident	Action Taken
Thurs.	10/12	Per. 1	fell asleep in class	parent contact note
Wed.	10/18	Per. 3	cut class	detention, call home
Wed.	10/18	Per. 7	smoking in lavatory	in-school suspension
Fri.	10/27	—	truant	assigned social worker
Mon.	10/30	Per. 1	under influence of alcohol	sent home by nurse

Notes: 10/12 Donna seemed exhausted - said she didn't sleep last night.
10/18 - Students reported that Donna was very upset and crying in lavatory.

Day	Date	Time	Parent Contact	Outcome
Thurs.	10/12	3 PM	sent note home	no response
Wed.	10/18	3 PM	called home	mother explained family problem
Fri.	10/30	3 PM	called home	father asked to be left alone

Notes: 10/13 Donna said she gave note to mother. 10/18 Complicated family problem reported to principal. 10/30 Father seemed very resentful of referral to social welfare agency—didn't know where Donna was.

Day	Date	Time	Referral	Outcome
Wed.	10/18	Per. 4	assistant principal	assigned detention
Wed.	10/18	Per. 8	principal	in-school suspension
Fri.	10/27	3 PM	principal	referral to social welfare agency

Notes: 10/18 Donna served detention. 10/19 Donna served suspension. 10/20 Donna asked guidance office about procedure to quit school. Meeting arranged to discuss Donna's problem with full professional staff.

Additional comments: Donna is 16 years old, and seems outwardly quite mature and self-confident. She is well liked by her classmates, and always shows her teachers respect and courtesy. Donna seems indifferent to the authority of the school—she breaks the rules and accepts punishment with equal ease. Her records indicate bright normal intelligence and no physical handicaps. Donna has been retained twice before, mainly due to frequent absence and failure to make up missed classwork and homework. She has refused to take exams. Donna participates in class discussions, and brings an almost adult perspective to many issues. She is rarely prepared with homework, and her frequent absences interfere with the continuity of instruction.

Teachers are on the front lines in the battle against child neglect and abuse. Knowing the facts, it would have been unreasonable to expect the girl in the preceding example to have given her total attention and concentration to schoolwork. Looking beyond the facts at hand, reserving judgment, following up with parent contacts and referrals, and demonstrating a genuine willingness to help can clear the path for effective instruction. Children frequently turn to their teachers as the only adults to whom they can relate their problems. Teachers should acquaint themselves with the kinds of resources and support services they can make available to their students in need.

General Health

Here are a few of the different kinds of problems which may interfere with learning in any classroom. Use the checklists which follow to structure your observations. Make referrals to appropriate professional staff members when patterns of related problems suggest that learning is being hampered, or if specific difficulties recur with sufficient frequency to warrant further evaluation.

Teacher's Guide to Vision Problems with Checklist (American Optometric Association). To aid teachers in detecting the children who should be referred for complete visual analysis, the American Optometric Association Committee on Visual Problems in Schools has compiled a list of symptoms—a guide to vision problems. The committee recommends:

1. That all children in the lower third of the class, particularly those with ability to achieve above their percentile rating, be referred for complete visual analysis.

2. That all children in the class who, even though achieving, are not working within reasonable limits of their own capacity be referred for a complete visual analysis.

Following are other symptoms which may indicate a visual problem, regardless of results in any screening test:

Observed in Reading

_____ Dislike for reading and reading subjects.
_____ Skipping or rereading lines.
_____ Losing place while reading.
_____ Slow reading and word calling.
_____ Poor perceptual ability, such as confusing *o* and *a*; *n* and *m*; etc.

Other Manifestations

_____ Restlessness, nervousness, irritability, or other unaccountable behavior.
_____ Desire to use finger or marker as pointer while reading.
_____ Avoiding close work.

_____ Poor sitting posture and position while reading.
_____ Vocalizing during silent reading, noticed by watching lips or throat.
_____ Reversals persisting in grade two or beyond.
_____ Inability to remember what has been read.
_____ Complaint of letters and lines "running together" or of words "jumping."
_____ Holding reading closer than normal.
_____ Frowning, excessive blinking, scowling, squinting, or other facial distortions while reading.
_____ Excessive head movements while reading.
_____ Writing with face too close to work.
_____ Fatigue or listlessness after close work.
_____ Inattentiveness, temper tantrums, or frequent crying.
_____ Complaint of blur when looking up from close work.
_____ Seeing objects double.
_____ Headaches, dizziness, or nausea associated with use of the eyes.
_____ Body rigidity while looking at distant objects.
_____ Undue sensitivity to light.
_____ Crossed eyes—turning in or out.
_____ Red-rimmed, crusted, or swollen lids.
_____ Frequent sties.
_____ Watering or bloodshot eyes.
_____ Burning or itching of eyes or eyelids.
_____ Titling of head to one side.
_____ Tending to rub eyes.
_____ Closing or covering one eye.
_____ Frequent tripping or stumbling.
_____ Poor hand and eye coordination.
_____ Thrusting head forward.
_____ Tension during close work.

Hearing (Bond, Tinker, and Wasson, 1979)
_____ Inattention during listing activities.
_____ Frequent misunderstanding of oral directions or numerous requests for repetition of statements.
_____ Turning one ear toward the speaker or thrusting head forward when listening.
_____ Intent gaze at the speaker's face or strained posture while listening.

_____ Monotone speech, poor pronunciation, or indistinct articulation.
_____ Complaints of earache or hearing difficulty.
_____ Insistence on closeness to sound sources.
_____ Frequent colds, discharging ears, or difficult breathing.

Speech

_____ Pitch too high or too low.
_____ Speaks in a monotone.
_____ Speech too loud or too soft.
_____ Speech too rapid or too slow.
_____ Stuttering or other difficulties with fluency of speech.
_____ Lisping or other misarticulations.
_____ Faulty breath control or nasality.

Health

_____ Absent from school frequently.
_____ Lack of energy.
_____ Obvious physical handicap or injury.
_____ Hidden physical handicap or injury.
_____ Injury, illness, or handicapping condition treated or controlled by medication.
_____ Injury, illness, or handicapping condition corrected by means of prescription lens, hearing aid, brace, or other device.
_____ Abnormally rapid weight loss or gain.
_____ Problems with teeth or gums.
_____ Other somatic complaints which recur with unusual frequency.

Checklist of Symptoms of Psychological Problems

Emotional Instability

_____ Tires easily.
_____ Passivity, restlessness, or shyness.
_____ Stubborn or uncooperative.
_____ Irritable or aggressive.
_____ Unable to assume responsibility.
_____ Inattentive or forgetful.
_____ Overly dependent on teacher.
_____ Nail biting, scratching, or constant body movements.

Graham and Robinson

Environmental Distractions

_____ Nervousness or insecurity.
_____ Lack of interests in schoolwork.
_____ Incomplete home study assignments.

Mental Immaturity

_____ Language immaturity.
_____ Lacks muscular coordination.
_____ Timidity or insecurity.
_____ Poor memory or attention span.
_____ Overly dependent on teacher.

Social Maladjustment

_____ Withdrawn, fearful, or nervous.
_____ Unaccustomed to responsibility.
_____ Insubordinate or hostile toward authority figures.
_____ Poor grooming or inappropriate dress.
_____ Few or no friends.

Objective observation of classroom behavior can yield a wealth of diagnostic and therapeutic information. Anecdotal information may also serve to document a need for referral for care not ordinarily provided by the school. Only the classroom teacher is in a position to observe a student's behavior on a daily basis, and to identify problems as they develop. Early intervention is often the most important ingredient in getting physical or psychological problems solved. Left untreated, these problems can interfere with the development of reading and study skills essential to academic success. Accomplishing our primary goal of developing independent learners may occasionally demand participation in activities which are not specifically instructional in nature. Our responsibility is the education of the whole individual—meeting each individual's needs as they arise. It would be unprofessional to ignore the reality of special physical or psychological needs.

Cultural Background

Teachers are well advised to draw upon the powerful forces which have shaped students throughout their lives. It is a great mistake to assume that no distance exists between reader and writer simply because you have controlled certain factors within the "artificial" environment of the classroom. We must understand, accept, respect, and make use of the forces which have been effective in educating our students outside the classroom. Students need to be encouraged to bring their backgrounds to school—to share their diverse customs and holidays. Learning is enriched by sharing multicultural backgrounds.

A third grade teacher from Brooklyn, New York related this example: Vasiliki had told the class about Greek Independence Day, a holiday her Greek-American family celebrated in March. The parade through Manhattan, the costumes and dancing, the music and songs in her native language, and a great list of foods were described in detail. The holiday, she explained, marks the anniversary of Greek independence from 400 years of Turkish rule.

Later in the term when news came that Turkey had annexed the island republic of Cyprus, with its large Greek-Cypriot population, the teacher and the class were better prepared to understand Vasiliki's strong concern. The class had learned to respect Vasiliki's culture, and to examine the issues of a crisis in world events with a real concern for the outcome.

A fifth grade teacher from a suburban community provided this example: There are very few times when a teacher should challenge a student's cultural background. One such unusual incident was related by an elementary classroom teacher from an affluent suburban community. The teacher noticed that two of his fifth grade girls seemed to have an unusual relationship. Although they shared a common surname, Sandy and Debra didn't behave at all as sisters—Debra seemed to cater to Sandy's every whim. Sandy's parents were diplomats in exile from a Far Eastern country in which slavery is practiced. The girl who shared Sandy's surname and address was not her sister, but (was) her slave. The classroom teacher was the first to discover this fact, and to communicate the "common knowledge" that slavery is not permitted in America.

General Knowledge

General knowledge is the set of information and ideas which individuals retain as a result of their experiences and insights. Individuals differ in their abilities to retain information and ideas, to perceive relationships and make inferences, and in their overall cognitive development. People also differ in the experiences they have

Graham and Robinson

had within a given environment as well as in the experiences they have had in crossing cultural, economic, and other socially determined boundaries. The level of general knowledge shared by the group of students in your classroom can be considered the least common denominator upon which to base your instructional program.

The teacher should anticipate a great range of individual differences among students. Some teachers and administrators evaluate the intelligence of their students on the basis of standardized test performance. Although these tests are attempts to measure general knowledge objectively, students with limited or diverse experiential backgrounds are often credited (erroneously) with limited intellectual capacity. When setting study goals for your students, don't let test scores alone determine your expectations. Reserve judgment until you have seen for yourself the kinds of work your students can do within the class setting.

Teacher expectation can make a big difference in how well students learn. In one experiment, teachers were assigned to teach "honors" classes. The classes, they were told, were comprised of intellectually gifted children. The fact is that the classes were comprised of "average" children, having "average" intellectual capacity. By the end of the term, however, the "honors" classes had learned significantly more than other average classes taught by teachers with average expectations. The honors teachers expected more, and got more!

Language Processing Skills

The degree to which learners have acquired oral language skills will probably have a bearing on students' study abilities. Fluent readers have developed the ability to be flexible in receiving and/or expressing the written form of language. Beginners or inexperienced readers, by comparison, are relatively rigid in the strategies they can draw upon in order to make sense out of printed words. Many students need help in developing flexible strategies for following the flow of written language. Even fluent readers need specific help for specific problems and particular writing tasks.

The checklists and procedures which follow have been useful to a number of teachers both as assessment devices and as structures for helping students get ready for study reading. Try them with your students early in the year. Adapt them to your needs. Use them to help students marshal their linguistic abilities for the tasks at hand.

Self-appraisal study checklist. Often, students are aware of their own personal difficulties in following the flow of written language. Many students try, unsuccessfully, to use one set of skills to complete a wide variety of assignments. Thomas and Robinson suggest that "our students' own requests for help have much to tell us." A simple checklist, like the one which follows (Thomas and Robinson, 1979, p. 1), can add to your other observations and insights. Be alert for evidence of inflexibility in your students' language processing skills.

What Study Tips Will Help You Have a Good Year?

What kinds of study tips will help you have a good year? Students often mention the factors listed as playing a part in their achievement. Please check the factors you think will help you. Your teacher will consider your requests carefully and will use this information to help you have a good year.

Check Your
Requests Here

1. I often need help in understanding the meanings of words. ☐

2. I often need help in understanding what I read. ☐

3. I need help because it takes me so long to read my assignments. ☐

4. I need help in telling the difference between what is important and what is unimportant as I am reading. ☐

5. I should like to have help in taking notes when I read an assignment. ☐

6. I need help in bringing ideas I have gained from reading together into a final paper or oral report. ☐

7. I find it difficult to become really interested in what I am reading. ☐

8. I need help in organizing my time so that I can get my work finished when it is due without last minute worry. ☐

9. I need help in concentrating. ☐

10. I am not aware of any special difficulties. ☐

What else can you think of that will help you have a good year? Please write your requests below.

_____

_____

_____

_____

Teacher observation checklist. Here is another checklist used to informally gather information about students. This checklist is used to

Graham and Robinson

record teacher observations about the language processing skills of their students.

Checklist of Teacher Observations on Students' Reading (From *Reading Diagnosis Kit* by Wilma H. Miller, copyright 1978 by The Center for Applied Research in Education, Inc. Published by The Center for Applied Research in Education, Inc., New York. Reprinted by permission of Prentice-Hall, Inc.)

Name _____ Class _____ Teacher _____

I. Overall Comprehension Strategies
   A. Is able to answer factual questions.
      Example: What is the duodenum? _____
   B. Is able to answer questions calling for inferring, drawing conclusions, drawing generalizations, summarizing, and reading between the lines.
      Example: Why do you think that deciduous teeth sometimes are called "milk teeth?" _____
   C. Is able to answer critical or evaluative questions.
      Example: Do you believe that a teenager who has crooked teeth should see an orthodontist? Why or why not? _____
   D. Is able to evaluate such propaganda techniques as the halo effect, the bandwagon effect, glittering generalities, testimonials, and emotionally-toned words. _____
   E. Is able to follow up content reading in a problem-solving situation such as an oral book report, a written book report, an experiment, creative dramatics, role playing, or creative writing. _____

II. Study Skills
   A. Finding the Main Idea
      1. Is able to locate a topic sentence in a paragraph. _____
      2. Is able to put a directly stated main idea in a paragraph in his/her own words. _____
      3. Is able to state an implied main idea of a paragraph in her/his own words. _____
      4. Is able to state the main idea of a longer passage. _____
   B. Significant Details
      1. Is able to locate significant details in a paragraph when necessary. _____
      2. Is able to locate the irrelevant details in a paragraph as an aid in finding those that are relevant to a specific idea. _____
   C. Organizational Skills
      1. Is able to outline a section or a chapter of a content textbook using main headings and subheadings. _____
      2. Is able to take notes from a content textbook. _____
      3. Is able to summarize a section or entire selection from a content textbook in her/his own words. _____
   D. Following Directions
      1. Is able to understand directions. _____
      2. Is able to follow directions in sequence. _____
   E. Location of Information
      1. Can use text aids effectively such as the table of contents, index, and glossary. _____
      2. Can locate information using reference material. _____
   F. Graphic Aids
      1. Can interpret maps, charts, tables, and diagrams. _____
      2. Can relate them to printed information. _____

III. Vocabulary Skills
  A. Context Clue Usage
     1. Has a cadry of context clue strategies to use. _____
     2. Is able to apply context clue usage effectively in determining the meanings of unknown words in tradebooks or content textbooks. _____
  B. Dictionary and Glossary Usage
     1. Can use the dictionary or the glossary in a textbook effectively in locating the pronunciation and meaning of unknown words which are met in a content textbook or tradebook. _____
     2. Is able to apply alphabetical sequence. _____
     3. Is able to use guide words. _____
     4. Is able to use the pronunciation key. _____
     5. Is able to choose the correct dictionary definition for use in the context of the unknown word. _____
  C. Sight Word Recognition
     1. Has a good stock of general vocabulary terms which can be recognized at sight. _____
     2. Has a good stock of specialized vocabulary terms in a content area which can be recognized at sight. _____
  D. Phonic Analysis
     1. Is able to use phonic analysis to determine the pronunciation and meaning of unknown general vocabulary terms when necessary. _____
     2. Is able to use phonic analysis to determine the pronunciation and meaning of specialized vocabulary terms in a content area when necessary. _____
  E. Structural Analysis
     1. Is able to use a base or root word to determine the pronunciation and meaning of unknown general or specialized vocabulary terms when necessary. _____
     2. Knows the meaning of common prefixes and can use them in determining the pronunciation and meaning of unknown general or specialized vocabulary terms. _____
        Examples: a, ante, anti, bi, circum, con, de, dis, ex, in, non, post, pre, pro, re, sub, trans, and un.
     3. Knows the meaning of common suffixes and can use them in determining the pronunciation and meaning of unknown general or specialized vocabulary terms. _____
        Examples: able, en, hood, less, ness, er, ment, and ward.
     4. Can identify appropriate meaning of words by placement of accent. _____
        Example: re' cord, re cord'.
     5. Can correctly divide general and specialized vocabulary terms into syllables for writing needs. _____

Readiness for Study Tasks

The concept of readiness is not limited to the primary grades. It is of tremendous importance that teachers across the grades help students establish readiness for study. You can ensure that your students will be ready to learn while you have them in your classroom, but once they take study assignments home they're on their own. If you notice that your students

- forget to complete their home assignments,
- don't have time to fit every subject in,
- rarely finish the assignments they start,
- find it difficult to do schoolwork at home,

then help them organize their personal study. Good study habits in the classroom may not carry over to the home study situation. You may have to enlist the aid of your students' parents until students have learned to take responsibility for getting homework done on their own. Here are three basic pointers to get them started in the right direction:

1. Make sure you understand what must be done and when it is due.
2. Budget your time (make a plan and stick to it).
3. Work efficiently (see your plan through).

Students who take your suggestions will have a framework for the development of mature study habits. The techniques which follow can help them get off to a good start.

Although our seventh grader, Paul, is used as an example, the suggestions which follow may be applied throughout the elementary school as well. Primary students should start to take responsibility for their own planning of study time.

Assignments. An assignment sheet, such as the one shown, can be distributed to students. The teacher can help the students by showing them how the sheet is organized, by putting homework on the chalkboard in this format, and by seeing that the students write down and understand their assignments before they go home.

Subject	English	Due 5/ 6/ 84
Read or study	Vocbulary Unit 12	
Write or do	Exercises 1 and 2	
Bring home	Vocabulary Book	

Subject	Math	Due 5/ 6/ 84
Read or study	Chapter 14	
Write or do	Ditto Sheet on Percentages	
Bring home	Ditto and Math Book	

Subject	Health	Due 5/ 7/ 84
Read or study	Drugs and Alcohol Unit	
Write or do	Ditto Questions Related to Readings	
Bring home	Book and Ditto	

Subject _____ Due ___ ___ ___
Read or study _____
Write or do _____
Bring home _____

Teacher's comments   Paul's health report topic is amphetamines.
Parent's comments/questions   Paul is still a bit confused about percentages and
            decimal fractions.

Teachers' and/or parents' comments are optional. For students requiring special attention the assignment sheet can be used for regular communication between teachers and parents.

Study schedule. A study schedule can be prepared, duplicated, and distributed to students. Ask the students to record the activities they engage in after school for one week. With the completed forms, the teacher can help individual students find a suitable block of time for completing home-study assignments each day of the week. Compromises should be sought which reflect the students' priorities.

Time	Monday	Tuesday	Wednesday	Thursday	Friday
3 - 4 PM	(Street			(Study)	Off
4 - 5 PM	Hockey	(Study)	(Study)	(Study)	Off
5 - 6 PM	Games)	(Study)	(Study)	(Baseball	Off
6 - 7 PM		(Guitar Lesson)		Game)	Off
7 - 8 PM	(Study)	(Baseball	(Religious	(Swim	Off
8 - 9 PM	(Study)	Game)	Instruction)	Team	Off
9 - 10 PM				Practice)	Off
10 - 11 PM					Off

Once the schedule has been set, examine the block of time set aside for homework and prepare a study budget.

Study Budget

Paul Subject	Time		Lori Subject	Time
English	7:00 - 7:45		Math	7:00 - 7:20
Break	7:45 - 8:00		Health	7:20 - 7:40
Health	8:00 - 8:30		Break	7:40 - 8:00
Break	8:30 - 8:40		English	8:00 - 8:30
Math	8:40 - 9:00			

Graham and Robinson

Emphasize the desirability of taking short breaks between subjects, and completing assignments in an order which is in keeping with the learner's style of working. Paul, for example, does his longest assignments first; Lori likes to get her easy assignments out of the way before she tackles the work she finds hardest. The study budget should change on a daily basis, depending upon the work to be completed. The students should be encouraged to explore different arrangements until they discover their own favorite style.

Organizing the task. Encourage good work habits and provide a good learning environment in your classroom as an example to the students of what to strive for when establishing their own place to work. Distribute a supplies checklist, such as the one below, which can be taped to an empty coffee can to serve as a desk or tabletop organizer. This will help store the supplies and keep them handy, especially when a dining table must do double duty as a study center, or when students share one desk.

Personal Property of

_____	Pens	_____	Stapler and Staples
_____	Pencils	_____	Glue
_____	Eraser	_____	Scissors
_____	Ruler	_____	Crayons or Markers
_____	Tape	_____	Pencil Sharpener

The student should be encouraged to seek out other supplies as they become necessary. A dictionary, thesaurus, encyclopedia, atlas, or almanac may be called for in some home study assignments. The learner should know what is available at home so that appropriate plans may be made to use the school or public library as necessary. The teacher should keep in mind that homework is meaningful so long as it can be accomplished by the students independently, as application or extension of classroom work. Be careful about making assumptions when it comes to homework. There are many factors at play outside the classroom. Formal, teacher-directed readiness activities are especially necessary when students are insecure about functioning independently with something new, or when they are confronted with complex material beyond their previous experience, and especially when students have not learned techniques for helping themselves get ready to learn.

Miss De Gregoris was preparing a lesson which included the reading of a short story about a family's experiences with a sea otter. De Gregoris was relatively certain that few, if any, of her students were familiar with the sea otter. Her students would need some experience in order to relate to the story.

Taking the class to the sea otter's habitat, or bringing a sea otter to class for direct experience with the animal, was not feasible since the students lived far from the sea otter's habitat and no individual specimen was available to the class. A study trip to the zoo was considered but the zoo had not yet acquired a sea otter. The natural history museum, however, did have an exhibit of the sea otter in its natural habitat.

Prior to their museum visit, De Gregoris showed the class a segment from a motion picture about the ecology of shellfish, in which sea otters were shown feeding on oysters. In the library vertical file, she found still photographs of sea otters which had been clipped from various magazines. She showed these to the class, along with encyclopedia photographs. Written and verbal descriptions of the sea otter accompanied the presentation at the museum. When the story was read, the students were truly ready to learn.

Conclusion

In the broadest sense, printed words have no meaning except that which the reader brings to the page. As teachers, our job is to focus what the student already knows about the writer's topic upon the reading task at hand. Getting students ready to read helps maximize the effectiveness of the educational experiences you provide.

Your knowledge and understanding of your students should help you to formulate realistic yet challenging educational goals, both in the long and the short term. Experiences and interactions must be designed in ways which demonstrate an understanding and acceptance of the learner as a human being, yet still provide a challenge to the learner to grow as a student.

The skills and strategies described in this handbook bring reader and writer together. This process requires an ongoing assessment of student abilities and needs before, during, and after reading.

The organization of Chapters 2-4 is based on three large categories: 1) before the eyes meet the page, 2) while the eyes are on the page, and 3) after the eyes leave the page. Large general approaches are spelled out in each category and then more specific, tied-to-grade-level techniques are illustrated.

Reaction Guide

Part I. What did the writer say? (check three)

_____ Reading specialists and other specially trained experts are the only teachers qualified to conduct diagnostic and prescriptive instruction in reading and study skills.

_____ The important differences between teachers have to do with how they teach, not what they teach.

_____ Most educational programs hinge upon the teacher's ability to help students move from where they are now toward a goal of higher achievement. The first step in the process involves offering each learner a realistic challenge to make a desired change.

_____ The distance between reader and writer may be viewed as the amount and type of new information and ideas confronting the learner about to study a given reading selection.

_____ In the broadest sense, printed words have no meaning.

Part II. What did the writer mean? (check three)

_____ A teacher's influence should extend beyond the classroom.

_____ Teachers must be very much aware of their own attitudes.

_____ All students are capable of achieving top grades.

_____ Teachers must not harbor prejudices.

_____ Content area teachers need not concern themselves with reading readiness.

Part III. How can we use the meaning?

1. Use the information about Donna provided in the *anecdotal log* to complete the *Checklist of Symptoms of Psychological Problems.* As Donna's teacher, which professional staff member(s) would you contact? Why? _____

_____

_____

What might you have done to help Donna in class? _____

_____

2. The school psychologist has informed you that Michael's verbal IQ score on a recent evaluation was 80. You have been told that this score indicates that Michael has limited intellectual capacity and you

have been asked to "go easy" with him. You observe that Michael is capable of completing almost any classwork assignment, but he "falls apart" during tests. You are Michael's teacher. What should you do?

_____

_____

3. Kerry was a straight *A* student all through elementary school, but since she has entered junior high school her average has dropped to a *C*. She is frequently late in submitting written work, yet Kerry's parents insist that she studies for hours after school. They are concerned about her grades. You are Kerry's teacher. What should you do?

_____

_____

_____

III. answers will vary   II. √   I.

Answers:

Graham and Robinson

Chapter 2
BEFORE THE EYES MEET THE PAGE

Structured Overview

Each of the terms in the following diagram is explained in Chapter Two. Familiarize yourself with the diagram and skim the chapter before reading. Complete the structured overview by drawing lines between related terms in the diagram before or during your skimming of the chapter. Change answers if you change your mind. To see how one group completed this preorganizer, turn to the end of Chapter Two.

What the teacher and students do prior to the actual study of a given piece of material is basic to, and potentially as important as, the study job itself. Prestudy activity is of extreme significance when a student is called upon to process information in print which is new or complex. The printed words can only take on meaning when the reader has some kind of related, organized experience to bring to the words. Building a sufficient body of prestudy experience, and organizing this experience in anticipation of a specific study task, can help learners find the meaning of the printed words they read.

As they mature, students should gradually require less teacher direction in order to complete challenging study tasks. Mature readers are those who have learned to do for themselves what their teachers had previously done for them:

1. generate clearly defined purposes for reading;
2. acquire sufficient experiences in order to anticipate both the *content* or subject matter of the reading material and the *process* by which the writer conveys the content; and
3. conduct an active dialogue with the writer resulting in adequate comprehension in relation to the purposes for reading.

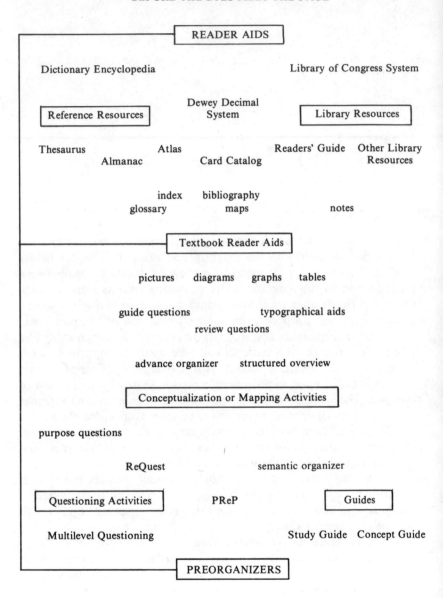

BEFORE THE EYES MEET THE PAGE

READER AIDS

Dictionary Encyclopedia

Library of Congress System

Reference Resources

Dewey Decimal
System

Library Resources

Thesaurus   Atlas   Readers' Guide   Other Library
          Almanac   Card Catalog   Resources

                    index   bibliography
              glossary   maps   notes

Textbook Reader Aids

        pictures   diagrams   graphs   tables

    guide questions   typographical aids
                    review questions

        advance organizer   structured overview

Conceptualization or Mapping Activities

purpose questions

            ReQuest   semantic organizer

Questioning Activities   PReP   Guides

Multilevel Questioning   Study Guide   Concept Guide

PREORGANIZERS

The examples you provide will serve as models of mature reading for your students to emulate.

Questions and Answers

Q. Why should subject area teachers take class time to teach students about the study process?

A. There comes a time when students must be weaned from depending upon their teachers for help they don't really need. This is as true of study help as any other kind. And it is true that students often have the ability to complete your assignments on their own, in which case direct teaching is unnecessary. But when they really don't know how to complete your assignments, you must step in and show them how. In this way, all teachers are reading teachers from time to time.

Q. My subject is complex, and broad in scope. How am I to provide all the prestudy experience my students need?

A. Students often have a vast store of direct and vicarious experiences to bring to any new learning situation. Unfortunately, many have not organized their experiences in ways which allow them ready access when problems arise. This may explain why high school teachers often suspect poor preparation in the junior high school (as junior high school teachers often suspect poor preparation in the elementary school) when students can't recall the experiences they have been provided. Teachers at all levels must both help students organize the experiences they have had, and provide experiences as necessary to make learning meaningful.

Q. How should I know what experiences and abilities my students need?

A. Use your experience as a teacher and as a mature reader to answer the following question:
What specific steps should my students take to efficiently complete the task I have assigned? The number of steps on your list may surprise you—even for a routine assignment. As you get to know your students, you should be able to identify the kinds of items they can and can't handle on their own. Tailor the suggestions which follow to provide them with custom-fit study assignments.

The Cone of Experience

Dale's Cone of Experience (From *Audiovisual Methods in Teaching*, 3rd edition, by Edgar Dale. Copyright (c) 1969 by Holt, Rinehart and Winston. Reprinted by permission of Holt, Rinehart and Winston, CBS College Publishing.) shows a variety of experiences which may be employed to develop readiness for a specific learning situation. The cone is organized in a way that shows the more concrete experiences (such as Direct Purposeful) providing a base, or support, for the more abstract experiences (such as Visual and Verbal Symbols). The teacher who provides direct and vicarious experiences such as these helps students get ready to learn.

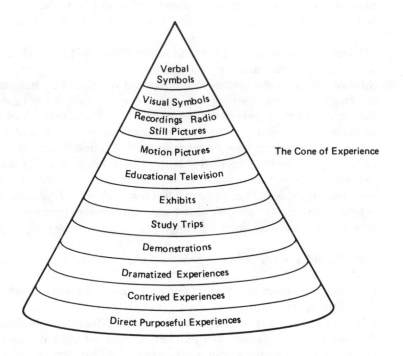

The Cone of Experience

Example: If students are to read about the specific operations of the 747 aircraft, and have only seen one in a movie, they may need to mobilize and organize experience at a concrete level before reading. The best concrete experience would be for the teacher to buy the class tickets and take them on a flight! Failing the ability or finances to undertake such a venture, the teacher could plan a visit to the airport and perhaps get a prior invitation to board. Or a dramatized class version of activities in a 747 could be organized by those with experience. Other alternatives are TV programs, motion pictures, and still pictures. The more concrete and specific the activity, the more students can mobilize for the reading task ahead.

Locating Information

Many teachers would be delighted to spend the term providing their students with direct, purposeful learning experiences, but find it impractical or impossible to do so on a daily basis. While teachers cannot realistically be expected to provide students with all the experiences they may need all the time, they can show students how to locate sources of experience-building information on their own. Students at all levels should be shown how to use textbook reader aids, reference resources, and library resources to locate the information they need to make the meaning of the printed words clear. Here's a checklist of information sources all students should learn to use:

TEXTBOOK READER AIDS

_____ table of contents	_____ pictures	_____ guide questions
_____ glossary	_____ diagrams	_____ review questions
_____ index	_____ maps	_____ typographical aids
_____ bibliography	_____ graphs	
_____ notes	_____ tables	

REFERENCE RESOURCES

_____ dictionary	_____ atlas
_____ encyclopedia	_____ almanac
_____ thesaurus	

LIBRARY RESOURCES

_____ Dewey Decimal System	_____ Readers' Guide
_____ Library of Congress System	_____ other library resources
_____ card catalog	

Let's now focus on each of the three areas: textbook reader aids, reference resources, and library resources. Each area is broken down into its parts with specific strategies delineated.

Textbook Reader Aids

All students read and study textbooks. Writers of textbooks are aware of the range of individual differences among readers, and provide reader aids as necessary to make the meaning of the printed words clear to the broadest possible audience. Textbooks which would otherwise be inappropriate for independent use by less mature readers become more "readable" once students have learned how to use the various parts of the textbook, graphic and typographic aids, and guide and review questions.

Commercial books, kits, and filmstrips for teaching students how to use parts of textbooks are available from a variety of sources. Whether selecting commercially prepared materials or preparing your own, be sure they include:

- where each part is located
- how it is organized
- what it is used for, and
- practical suggestions for independent use.

The following are some examples of materials for showing students how to locate information in textbooks. They can be used as initial lessons, or some of them might be used directly for older students.

Table of contents (Robinson & Hall, 1980, p. 8). A table of contents gives the author's plan for the book and how it is divided. It names the main parts of the book. In this way, you get the idea of the topics and subtopics the author has written about.

Directions: A table of contents is shown below. Use it to answer the 10 questions which follow.

1. On what page does the chapter "The Northwest Territory" begin?
2. What is the number of the unit in which the chapter "The Northwest Territory" appears?
3. On what page does the unit containing information on the Civil War begin?
4. On what page does the last chapter of that unit begin?
5. What is the title of the chapter in which you would probably find some information on railroads that connected eastern and western parts of the United States?
6. What is the title of the unit in which that chapter appears?
7. On what page does the unit begin?
8. How many pages are in the chapter entitled "A Vast New Land?"
9. What is the title of the chapter that probably tells how a favorite American holiday began?
10. What is the number of the unit in which that chapter appears?

The glossary. The glossary is a small, specialized dictionary located in the back of most textbooks. The glossary contains the meanings of words as they are used in the text, considered new or difficult for most readers. The words defined in a glossary are arranged in alphabetical order. The words at the top of each page in the glossary are called *guide words*. They tell the first and last words defined on that page. When you want to find the meaning of a new or difficult word used in a textbook, check the glossary (before reaching for a dictionary).

Directions: Study this sentence (from *Life: A Biological Science*, Newton Edition, by Paul E. Brandwein et al., © 1975 by

Harcourt Brace Jovanovich, Inc. Reprinted by permission of the publisher) and then answer the six questions which follow.

> *When human beings select the organisms they want to survive, they have introduced artificial selection.*

If you were unsure of the meaning of the term *artificial selection* as used in the sentence, you could turn to the glossary for its definition. You can quickly locate the exact page on which *artificial selection* is defined because words in a glossary are listed and defined in alphabetical order. The guide words at the top of each glossary page are your clues. The word on the top left is the first word defined on the page, and the word on the top right is the last.

1. Would the term *artificial selection* be found in the beginning, middle, or end of the glossary?
2. Here are guide words from the first three glossary pages:

Guide Words at the Top of Glossary   Page No.

Adaptation	Annuals	478
Antennas	Cilia	479
Ciliates	Endoskeleton	480

On which page would you expect to find the meaning of the term artificial selection? _____ Why?

3. Here is a sample glossary page.

antennae, projecting sense organs on the heads of insects and related invertebrates, 320
anther, the pollen-containing structures at the tip of the stamen of a flower, 263
antibiotics, substances produced by bacteria or fungi, used in medicine to stop the growth of disease microorganisms in the body, 216
arachnids, arthropods with four pairs of legs, mainly the spider, 281
archaeologist, a scientist who studies the life and culture of ancient peoples through artifacts and relics found in the earth
archegonium, the egg-producing organ in mosses and ferns, 226
arteries, blood vessels that carry blood away from the heart, 112
arthropods, major land-adapted invertebrates with jointed legs, including insects, spiders, and crabs, 318
artificial selection, the selection and breeding of particular plants and animals to produce offspring with desired traits, 456
ascospore, a type of fungal spore formed by sexual rather than asexual reproduction, 212
asexual reproduction, a form of reproduction in which a single parent produces offspring; fission, budding, and spore formation are common forms, 76

         Graham and Robinson

ATP (adenosine triphosphate), a cell substance that stores the energy from oxidation of glucose, and which releases the energy by releasing a phosphate group, thus making energy available to the cell, 183

auricle, in vertebrates, the chamber of the heart that receives blood from the veins and sends it to a ventricle, 94

auxin, a plant hormone that regulates growth, 190

Which word is defined before *artificial selection*? _____
After? _____ Why does *artificial selection* belong between these two words? _____

4. What does *artificial selection* mean? _____

5. On what page of the textbook is the meaning of *artificial selection* explained? _____

6. Can you think of any other sources of information about *artificial selection*? _____

The index. The index is a detailed listing of topics discussed in a textbook. It is usually found in the back of the book, and is arranged in alphabetical order by topic. The page number(s) on which a topic is discussed appear beside each topic in the index. When you are interested in locating information about a specific topic, check the index.

Directions: Study this partial index (from *Life: A Biological Science*, Newton Edition, by Paul F. Brandwein et al., © 1975 by Harcourt Brace Jovanovich, Inc. Reprinted by permission of the publisher.) and answer the questions which follow it.

baboon, 371
bacilli, **214**
Bacillus anthrax, **214**
backbone, 98, **99**, 341
bacteria, 73, 80, 200, **214**-217, 403;
   antibiotics made from, 216;
   decay, 15, 38, 60, 75, 216, 217;
   destroyed by white blood cells, 80, 215;
   flagellated, 280;
   harmful, 214-215; helpful, 216-217;
   intestinal, 216-217; nitrogen-fixing, 216;
   reproduction, 214-215; rod-shaped, **214**; round, **214**;
   spiral-shaped, **214**;
badger, 55, 56

1. Topics related to each main topic are listed alphabetically, with page numbers. How many topics are directly related to *bacteria*? _____

2. Page numbers in bold print are usually the best sources of information. Which page would probably have the best information about the shapes of *bacteria*? _____
3. The words "see also" direct you to other possible sources of information related to a topic in the index. For example, *blood*: circulation, **112-115, 116**; deoxygenated, **116; see also** red blood cells; white blood cells.

   Besides pages 112-116, where else might you look for more information about *blood*? _____
4. Suppose you were interested in learning more about germs. Besides *bacteria*, what other topics might you check in the index? _____

Bibliography. A bibliography lists the sources of information used in the writing of a textbook, alphabetically by the author's last name. There are different forms for writing a bibliography, but each bibliography will help you locate the sources of the textbook writer's ideas. A bibliography usually can be found in the back of a textbook, although some writers provide a bibliography of suggested readings after each chapter or unit. When you want to find out where writers get their information, check the bibliography.

Directions: Study the following bibliography from a political science text. Then answer the eight questions about the bibliography.

BIBLIOGRAPHY

(M. Edison & S.F. Heimann. *Public Opinion Polls.* New York: Franklin Watts, Inc., 1972, p. 59. Reprinted by permission of Franklin Watts, Inc.)

Boyd, Harper, W., Jr., and Westfall, Ralph. *Marketing Research, Text and Cases.* Homewood, Illinois: Richard D. Irwin, 1964.

Campbell, Angus, Converse, Philip E., Miller, Warren E., and Stokes, Donald E. *The American Voter.* New York: John Wiley & Sons, 1960.

Converse, Paul D., Huegy, Harvey W., and Mitchell, Robert V. *Elements of Marketing.* Englewood Cliffs, New Jersey: Prentice-Hall, 1958.

Converse, Philip E., and Schuman, Howard. "'Select Majorities' and the Vietnam War." *Scientific American*, Vol. 222 (June 1970).

Free, Lloyd A., and Cantril, Hadley. *The Political Beliefs of Americans: A Study of Public Opinion.* New Brunswick, New Jersey: Rutgers University Press, 1967.

Johnson, Norman L., and Smith, Harry, Jr., editors. *New Developments in Survey Sampling.* New York: Wiley-Interscience, 1969.

Slonim, Morris J. *Sampling in a Nutshell.* New York: Simon and Schuster (paperback), 1960.

Spiegelman, Mortimer. *Introduction to Demography.* Cambridge, Massachusetts: Harvard University Press, 1968.

White, Theodore H. *The Making of the President 1960.* New York: Atheneum Publishers, 1961 (also Pocket Books paperback).

Zeisel, Hans. *Say it with Figures.* New York: Harper and Row (Torchbook paperback), 1968.

1. Who wrote *Elements of Marketing*?
2. What book did Johnson and Smith edit?
3. Is *Scientific American* a book? If not, what is it?
4. When was *Say it with Figures* published?
5. Who published Slonim's book? In what form?
6. Where is Harvard University Press located?
7. Here is some mixed-up information. Reorganize it into a fictional entry based on the form in this bibliography:
   a. Prentice-Hall
   b. Ralph Johnson, Teresa Bonanno, and Alan Rhodes (editors)
   c. *How to Survey*
   d. Englewood Cliffs
   e. 1983
   f. New Jersey
8. Between which two entries in the bibliography would you place your new one?

Notes. Notes of different kinds are frequently found in texts—sometimes at the bottom of a page (footnotes), sometimes in side margins (sidenotes), and sometimes at the end of a chapter or unit (endnotes). Frequently, the information in a note cites the source of an author's words or ideas. At times notes may draw the reader's attention to supplementary information and sources for further study.

Directions: Study this sidenote from a section on the effects of drinking alcohol in a seventh grade health textbook (J.T. Fodor & others. *A Healthier You*. River Forest, Illinois: Laidlaw Brothers, 1980, p. 237. Reprinted by permission of Laidlaw Brothers, A Division of Doubleday & Company, Inc.) and answer the questions which follow it.

Cirrhosis of the liver and accidents are among the leading causes of death in the United States today. To find out how alcohol is related to cirrhosis of the liver and to accidents, write to: National Council on Alcoholism, 2 Park Avenue, New York, NY 10016, and National Safety Council, 425 North Michigan Avenue, Chicago, IL 60611.

1. What do you suppose was the author's purpose in providing this sidenote?
2. What sort of information does this sidenote provide?

Pictures. Black and white or colored paintings or sketches, cartoons, and/or photographs are provided throughout textbooks to help readers visualize subject matter. Most textbook pictures are captioned. The caption tells the reader what to look for in the picture, and how the picture is related to the printed words. Students should read the captions and study the pictures provided in textbooks to help make the meaning of the printed words clear. When readers need help in visualizing something in print, they should study any available pictures.

Directions: Study this picture and caption from a science textbook (S.S. Blanc, A.S. Fischler, & O. Gardner. *Modern Science: Earth, Space, and Environment.* New York: Holt, Rinehart and Winston, Inc., 1967, p. 14. Used by permission of Holt, Rinehart and Winston, Publisher.).

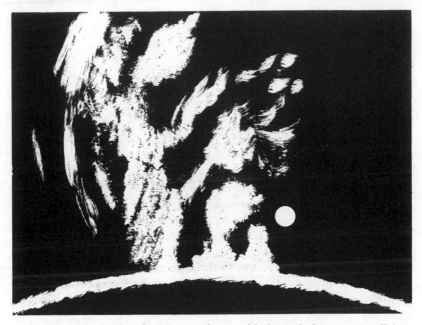

1-14   Compare the size of a solar prominence with the earth shown as a small dot.

1. What can you tell about the size of a solar prominence as compared with the size of the earth?

   _____

2. The dark, curved object at the bottom of the picture is the

   _____

3. Does the solar prominence appear to move away from or toward the surface of the sun? _____

   _____

Here is the printed part of the text which explains solar prominences.

Sometimes huge clouds of hot gases explode from the corona shooting out at speeds as high as 450 miles per second to a height of 250,000 miles (Fig. 1-14). These tremendous explosions are called *solar prominences* (prahm-ih-nens-uhz) and, like sunspots, have been found to give off strong radio waves and ultraviolet radiation which interfere with our radio and long distance telephone reception on earth.

4. With the additional information provided in the printed words, you should be able to determine:
   - The name for the ring of light surrounding the surface of the sun. _____
   - The direction and speed of the solar prominence. _____
   - The size of the solar prominence. _____
   - Other facts about the solar prominence which are not pictured. _____

Diagrams (Robinson & Hollander, 1980, p. 15). A diagram is a drawing that shows the important features, functions, or relationships of an idea the author(s) are trying to put across. It may also help us visualize what a thing is or how it works. It may have labels, captions, and illustrations that identify the important parts and their purposes.

You will understand how the United Nations System works after you have "read" the diagram that follows.

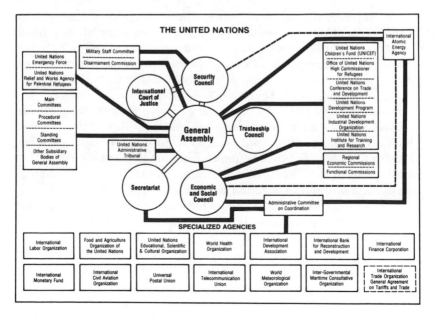

Directions: Following are nine incomplete statements about the system of the United Nations. You can complete each statement by carefully studying the diagram. Number each answer as you complete your answer sheet.

1. The International Court of Justice is responsible to the General Assembly and the _____.
2. The World Health Organization is responsible to the Administrative Committee on Coordination and the Economic _____.
3. There are _____ specialized agencies.
4. The Regional Economic Commissions are responsible to the _____.
5. The United Nations Relief and Works Agency for Palestine Refugees is responsible to the _____.
6. The Trusteeship Council is only responsible to the _____.
7. The abbreviation for the United Nations Children's Fund is _____.
8. The Disarmament Commission is responsible to the General Assembly and to the _____.
9. The United Nations Conference on Trade and Development is responsible to the General Assembly and to the _____.

Maps. Maps may be found anywhere a textbook writer needs to show the earth's surface in order to make the meaning of the printed word clear. Maps are drawn to scale, and are arranged according to the directions of the compass. Maps can be used to gain an understanding of the relative shapes, sizes, and importance of land areas and bodies of water. Maps are the best answer when the question is, "Where?"

Directions (J.H. Dempsey. *Let Freedom Ring: A History of the United States*, teacher's edition. Morristown, New Jersey: Silver Burdett Company, 1980, p. T32. Reprinted by permission of Silver Burdett Company.): Listed below are four important natural resources found in the United States. Listed also are five states in which each of these natural resources is found in large amounts. Use the symbols in the key to show this information on the outline map. You will need to draw more than one symbol in some states.

Graham and Robinson

Coal	Oil	Iron ore	Natural gas
West Virginia	Texas	Minnesota	Texas
Kentucky	Louisiana	Michigan	Louisiana
Pennsylvania	California	California	Oklahoma
Illinois	Oklahoma	Missouri	New Mexico
Ohio	Wyoming	Wyoming	Kansas

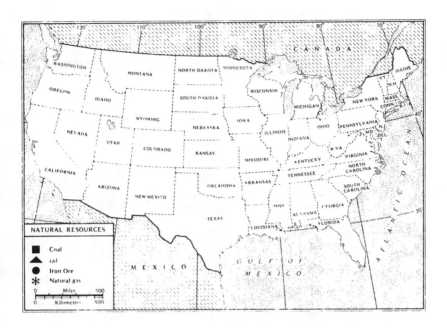

The legend, or key, explains the symbols used on each particular map. Concepts such as political boundaries, longitude and latitude, time zones, hemispheres, height above and below sea level, contour, compass direction, and scale of miles or kilometers may require explanation and practice in the form of exercises. The distortion which results from using a flat map to represent the curved surface area of the earth may also require explanation, particularly when the globe presents conflicting information.

Tables. Tables use rows and columns to list information in condensed form for ready access. Tables may be found anywhere a textbook writer wants to summarize important information, or they may appear as an appendix in the back of the book. Special symbols used in a table are usually explained in a key at the bottom of the table.

Students should be directed to look back and forth between the text of the selection and the table which summarizes the print.

Directions: Study the following chart. Then answer the 10 questions which follow.

BLADE SELECTION CHART

14 Teeth	To cut material 1″ diameter or over	Aluminum Brass Bronze Cast Iron	Copper Cold Rolled Steel Heavy Angles Soft Steel
18 Teeth	To cut material ¼″ to 1″ diameter	Angles, heavy Angles, light Cast iron Drill rod General cutting	Small solids Solid cold rolled steel stock, machined Tool steels
24 Teeth	To cut material ⅛″ to ¼″ diameter or thickness	Angles, light Brass pipe Brass tubing Heavy sheet metal Iron pipe	Metal conduit Sheet metal over 18 gauge Tubing over 18 gauge
32 Teeth	To cut material less than ⅛″ in thickness	Sheet metal under 18 gauge Tubing under 18 gauge	

(Reprinted from *Basic Metalwork*, Copyright 1978 by John L. Feirer and John R. Lindbeck. Used with permission of the publisher, Bennett Publishing Company, Peoria, Illinois 61615. All rights reserved.)

1. What kinds of information are summarized in this table?
2. "Soft or heavy metals require a coarse tooth blade while thin wall sections, such as tubing, require one with fine teeth." How many teeth are there in a coarse tooth blade? A fine tooth blade?
3. How are the different kinds of hacksaw blades arranged for comparison in this table?
4. Which blade would you choose to cut a piece of 2″ diameter aluminum stock?
5. An 18 tooth blade would be the correct choice to cut a ¾″ drill rod. True or False
6. Which two blades could be used to cut a ¼″ light angle?
7. In what units are sheet metals measured?

Graham and Robinson

8. Study the kinds of materials recommended to be cut with a 32 tooth blade. Is 18 gauge material greater than or less than ⅛" in thickness?
9. Which blade would you choose to cut heavy sheet metal?
10. Why are several kinds of hacksaw blades needed in metalwork?

Graphs. Graphs are used by textbook writers to compare quantities and show trends or patterns. The type of graph a textbook writer uses will depend upon the kinds of information being compared and the purpose the graph serves in illustrating the meaning of the printed words. Bar graphs and line graphs are similar in how they represent quantities. Circle or "pie" graphs represent each item as part of the whole collection of items under consideration. Be sure to find out what units of measurement are used in bar and line graphs, and what part of the whole collection of items under consideration is being represented.

Directions: Study this circle graph of the earth's minerals (from *Matter: Its Forms and Changes* by Paul F. Brandwein et al., © 1972 by Harcourt Brace Jovanovich, Inc. Reprinted by permission of the publisher).

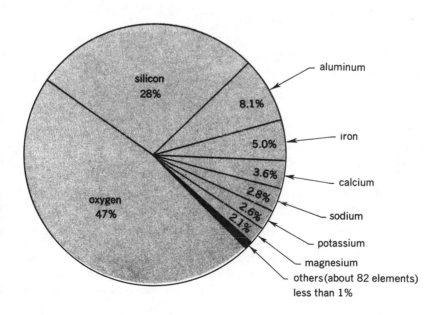

1. What portion of the earth's minerals is represented by this graph?
2. Which element accounts for about half of the earth's mineral resources?
3. Which element accounts for about one-quarter of the earth's mineral resources?

Directions: Study this bar graph of the elements of the earth (from *Matter: Its Forms and Changes* by Paul F. Brandwein et al., © 1972 by Harcourt Brace Jovanovich, Inc. Reprinted by permission of the publisher).

ELEMENTS OF THE EARTH

Element		Percentage by weight
oxygen		49.5
silicon		25.7
aluminum		7.5
iron, zinc, tin, copper, lead		4.73
hydrogen		.88
carbon		.09
nitrogen		.03
others		11.57

1. Which three elements together account for three-quarters of the earth's weight?
2. Which three elements together account for 1 percent of the earth's weight?
3. How much of the earth's weight is iron, zinc, tin, copper, and lead?
4. How do bar graphs and circle graphs differ in their presentation of similar information?

Questions and typographic aids. Writers of textbooks provide guide questions, review questions, and special typographic features to help readers identify the important information and ideas developed in the text. Guide questions let the reader know in advance which topics

Graham and Robinson

and issues the text will address. Readers may expect to find the answers to guide questions while they read.

This guide question is from a section in a social studies chapter about the United States after World War I (Sidney Schwartz and John R. O'Connor. *Exploring Our Nation's History, Volume 2: The Age of Greatness Since the Civil War.* Copyright 1971 by Globe Book Company, Inc. Used by permission.):

What were the causes of the great depression?

The subheadings in this section read as follows:
A. The Stock Market Crash
B. Overexpansion of Credit
C. An Unbalanced Economy
D. Sick Industries
E. Weakness of Labor Unions
F. Government Policies
G. The Election of 1932

The guide question and subheadings help the reader anticipate the direction of information and ideas presented by the writer. Other guide questions used in this section include:
• Why did the stock market crash?
• Why did the crash touch off such a terrible depression?

Review questions presented at the conclusion of a segment of text should actually be read in advance, so that students may know what information is considered most important to remember while they read. Here are a few review questions from the social studies section about the great depression:
1. Why did the stock market crash in October 1929?
2. Why was credit overexpanded in 1929?
3. Why did unemployment rise during the 1920s?

Reading these questions in advance of the section about the great depression can help learners anticipate the important information and ideas to be presented in the text. Speculating, or taking an "educated guess," about the correct answers to review questions before the actual reading of a section of text can help learners marshal their experiences. Taking a guess also represents an investment in learning— students who actively speculate about what they read are interested to find out if they have guessed correctly. They are also better motivated to find out why, if it turns out that their guesses were wrong.

Headings in boldface print, words in italics, dates, numbers, special symbols, underlining, color highlighting, and other outstanding typographic aids in print are intended to make important information stand out. Students can make outstanding typographic features into guide questions to be answered while reading the body of the text.

Activities such as making guide questions from typographic features in print involve the learner in purpose-setting. Purpose-setting and speculating are two independent study techniques employed by mature readers. Once learned, these techniques readily transfer to many reading and study situations. If the answer to the student's questions is not to be found in the text, then the situation may call for the use of reference resources.

Reference Resources

Reference resources can provide students with the base of experience they need in order to relate to new or different topics, concepts, and terminology. Teachers should not casually assume that their students know how to use even the common reference resources—dictionary, encyclopedia, thesaurus, atlas, almanac.

At some point in the development of their independent study skills, all students need to be shown the kind of information contained, and the way in which information is organized in each common reference source. Direct, systematic instruction in how to choose and use reference resources is most effective when conducted within the context of an ongoing study assignment. The appropriateness of a given reference source—a dictionary, for example—is determined by the purpose to which it is to be put, and the maturity of the individual user. Following are examples of materials for direct instruction in how to locate information in common reference resources.

The Dictionary. Be a Better Reader, Book I (Nila B. Smith. Englewood Cliffs, New Jersey: Prentice-Hall, Inc., 1963, p. 108), includes this section for junior high and high school students on how to find things quickly in the alphabetical index of a dictionary and how to use guide words.

Alphabetical Order and Guide Words

Finding a letter *quickly* in the alphabetical index of a dictionary is your first important dictionary skill. Follow the directions and answer the questions below to get more practice in this skill.

1. Write the letters of the alphabet in order:

_____

2. How many letters are there in the alphabet? _____
3. If the alphabet were divided in half, which letters would be in the first half?

_____

Making use of the Guide Words at the top of a page in a dictionary is another important skill. Instead of turning page after page in the section of *Ls* to find loam, you simply look at the top of the page, where the Guide Words might be *Lissiz-Loan*. You know that the beginning letters of *loam* are *loa* and that the last letter *m* comes before *n* as in *loan*. So, you decide at once that *loam* is on this page, and you find it quickly.

Here are some Guide Words that are at the top of certain pages in a dictionary.

Page 204   Bagatine—Bail
Page 1926   Position—Possession
Page 3852   Vitaglass—Vitrification

4. Underline the words in this list that you would find on page 204: baboon, baby, bagpipe, baffle, bait, baggy, bacteria, bald, Bahama, bucket.
5. Underline the words in this list that you would find on page 1926: positive, port, pore, pollen possess, pressure, posse, porcelain, profess.
6. Underline the words in this list that you would find on page 2852: vision, vitamin, vinegar, vital, vest, van, vitreous, vein, volcano.

Naturally, teachers may need to help students develop dictionary skills other than efficiently locating entries. The preceding lesson was written to help with the teaching of location skills; but your students may need to learn how to use the parts of a dictionary entry, or how to handle multiple meanings and multiple entries. Commerically prepared materials are often limited in scope or depth of skills development. Worksheets and other commercially prepared learning activities should be selected on the basis of how well they fit in with the teacher's specific goals and objectives for a specific group of learners.

Here are examples of other lessons for cultivating addditional dictionary skills.

Parts of a dictionary entry. Study the sample entries based on Thorndike & Barnhart, 1974, Scott, Foresman which follow. Parts have been numbered for ease of identification:

ig loo (ig lū), *n., pl.* -loos.　A dome shaped hut used by Eskimos, often built of blocks of snow. [<Eskimo *igdlu* house]—⑧

An igloo is a surprisingly warm shelter. ——⑨

The following kinds of information are provided about the word *igloo*:

1. the correct spelling of the entry word
2. the correct syllabication of the entry word
3. phonetic respelling for pronunciation
4. the part of speech of the entry word (n means that igloo is a noun)
5. variant forms of the entry word (*igloos* is the plural form of *igloo*)
6. the correct meaning of the entry word
7. an illustration of an *igloo*
8. the origin, or etymology, of the entry word (the English word igloo comes from the Eskimo word for house)
9. the correct usage of the entry word (an example of how the word *igloo* can be used in a sentence)

Pronunciation

gneiss (nis), n. any of various very dense rocks consisting of coarse layers of quartz and feldspar alternating with layers of any of several other minerals. [<German Gneis].

1. How many syllables can the word *gneiss* be divided into?
2. Circle the word that is pronounced the same as *gneiss*:
   niece   nice   gaze
   Use the phonetic pronunciation key in your dictionary to help you.
3. What part of speech is the word gneiss?
4. Use the word gneiss in a sentence which shows its meaning.

_____

5. What is the country of origin of the word *gneiss*?

Multiple Meanings
   Many words have more than one meaning.

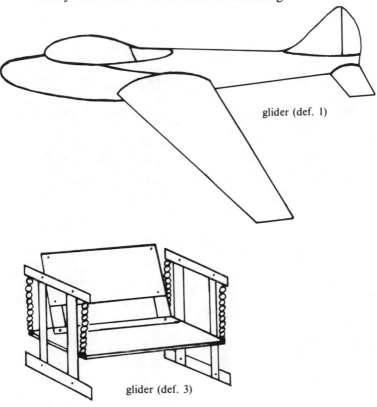

glider (def. 1)

glider (def. 3)

   glider (glī'dər), n.   1. a motorless aircraft that is kept in the air by rising air
   currents.   2. person or thing that glides.   3. a swinging seat suspended on a
   frame. Gliders are usually placed on porches or outdoors.

1. How many different meanings are given for the word *glider*?
2. Which meaning of *glider* do you think is most often used?
3. Why do you suppose there are two illustrations with this entry?

The Dictionary As an Encyclopedia
    Directions: Answer the questions by using the dictionary page as a miniature encyclopedia.

DICTIONARY PAGE (Robinson & Hall, 1980, p. 29)

May (mā), the fifth month of the year. It has 31 days. n.

Ma ya (mī'ə) 1. one of an ancient Indian people who lived in Central America and Mexico. The Mayas had a high degree of civilization from about A.D. 800, long before they were discovered by the Spaniards. 2. their language n. pl.

Ma yas. -Ma'yan, adj., n.

may be (mā'bē) it may be; possibly; perhaps: Maybe you'll have better luck next time. adv.

May Day the first day of May, often celebrated by crowning a girl honored as the queen of May, dancing around the maypole, etc. In some parts of the world, labor parades and meetings are held on May Day.

may flow er (mā'flou'ər) any of several plants whose flowers blossom in May, as the trailing arbutus (in the United States), and the hawthorn or cowslip (in England) n.

May flow er (mā'flou ər) ship on which the Pilgrims came to America.

may fly (mā'flī) a slender insect, having lacy front wings which are much larger than the hind wings. It dies soon after reaching the adult stage. n. pl. may flies.

may hap (mā' hap) old use, perhaps. adv.

may hem (mā' hem) crime of intentionally maiming a person or injuring him so that he is less able to defend himself. n.

may n't (mā'ənt) may not.

may on naise (mā'ə nāz) a salad dressing made of egg yolks, vegetable oil, vinegar or lemon juice, and seasoning, beaten together until thick. n.

may or (mā'ər) person at the head of a city or town government, chief official of a city or town. n.

may or al ty (mā'ər əl tē or mer'ər tē) 1. position of mayor. 2. mayor's term of office. n. pl. may or al ties.

may pole or *May pole* (mā' pōl') a high pole decorated with flowers or ribbons, around which merrymakers dance on May Day. n.

mayst (mast) Old Use, may, "Thou mayst" means "you may." v.

maze (māz) 1. network of paths through which it is hard to find one's way. A guide led us through a maze of caves. 2. state of confusion; muddled condition: He was in such a maze he couldn't speak. n.

ma zur ka (ma zer'kə or ma zur'kə). 1. a lively Polish dance. 2. music for it. n. pl. ma zur kas.

ma zour ka (mə zer'kə or mə zur'kə) mazurka n. pl. ma zour kas.

maz y (mā'ze) like a maze; intricate. adj. maz i er, maz i est.

M.C. Master of Ceremonies.

Mc Clellan (mə klel'ən) George B., 1826-1885. Union general in the Civil War. n.

Mc Cor mick (mə kôr'mik) Cyrus Hall, 1809-1884. American inventor of harvesting machinery. n.

Mc Kin ley (mə kin'lē) 1. William, 1843-1901, the 25th president of the United States, from 1897 to 1901. 2. Mount, mountain in Central Alaska, the highest peak in North America, n.

MD Maryland.

M.D. Doctor of Medicine.

me (mē) I and me mean the person speaking. She said, "Give the dog to me. I like it and it likes me." pron.

ME Maine.

mead[1] (mēd) meadow, n. [Old English, maed]

Meade (mēd) George Gordon, 1815-1872, Union general in the Civil War. n.

Graham and Robinson

1. What is a *maypole*?
2. When did the *Mayflower* come to America?
3. Where is *Mount McKinley* located?
4. Was *William McKinley* the 23rd or the 25th president of the United States?
5. Which abbreviation means *Doctor of Medicine*?
6. In what war did *General George Gordon Meade* take part?
7. When was *Cyrus McCormick* born?
8. What does the abbreviation *M.C.* mean?
9. Where did the *Mayas* live?
10. What interesting fact about *Mount McKinley* is given?
11. Did Generals Meade and McClellan fight on the same side during the Civil War?
12. What did *Cyrus McCormick* invent?
13. When was *William McKinley* president of the United States?
14. Name one way in which a young girl is honored on *May Day*?
15. Did the *Mayan* civilization flourish before the Spaniards discovered them?
16. Is *May Day* celebrated on the first or last day of May?

The encyclopedia. Learning to use the encyclopedia is doubly important for school-age learners. First, it is a convenient source of information on most any topic, written on a level even younger learners can understand on their own. In addition, gaining an understanding of how information is organized in an encyclopedia is an important first step toward independence with a variety of reference resources. Relating one system of organization (the alphabetical sequence of topics) to another (the numeric sequence of volumes) is a prerequisite for higher study skills such as locating information in library research.

The following are sample activities for developing encyclopedia skills. Having an encyclopedia in class when these skills are taught can provide an excellent opportunity for learning.

Improving Your Encyclopedia Skills

A	B	C	D	E	F	GH	IJ	KL	MN	OP	QR	S	TUV	W	XYZ
1	2	3	4	5	6	7	8	9	10	11	12	13	14	15	16

An encyclopedia is a set of volumes numbered in order. You can quickly find information on almost any topic by first selecting the correct volume and then, using the guide words, find the page(s) on which the topic is discussed. If the topic you are looking up is a person, be sure to look under the person's last name. For example, if you wanted information about Thomas A. Edison, you would select volume 5 of this encyclopedia because Edison begins with *E*, the letter of the alphabet treated in volume 5.

Selecting the Correct Volume

Directions: In the space provided, write the volume number you would select to find information on each of the following topics.

1. radiation _____	6. Indian Ocean _____
2. automobile _____	7. India _____
3. Louis Pasteur _____	8. torpedo _____
4. snakes _____	9. giraffe _____
5. volcanoes _____	10. computers _____

Cross-references

If you look up the topic *car* in an encyclopedia, you are very likely to get a message instead of the information you want. This message is called a *cross-reference*:

car, see *automobile*

This cross-reference means that the topic *car* is discussed under *automobile*, and that you should turn to the volume in which the automobile is discussed for the information you need. As you use the encyclopedia, you will find many cross-references. Sometimes the topic you look up will be found under a different name from the one you ordinarily use (like looking under *car* for *automobile*).

Another situation which calls for a cross-reference is when the topic you look up is a part of a larger topic:

Apollo 13, see *space travel*

This cross-reference means that information about *Apollo 13* is part of a larger topic called *space travel*. If you want to know more about *Apollo 13*, you will have to turn to the volume in which *space travel* is discussed. Many reference resources make use of cross-references to avoid having to repeat the same information in different places.

Directions: In the space provided, write the number of the encyclopedia volume in which you would find each of the following cross-references.

1. *Mahican Indians*, see *Mohican Indians* _____
2. *mail*, see *post office* _____
3. *mainspring*, see *clock* _____
4. *make up*, see *theater* _____, *motion picture* _____, *cosmetics* _____
5. *moray*, see *eel* _____

The thesaurus. A thesaurus is a book of synonyms and antonyms. Synonyms are words that have the same meaning. *Car* and *automobile* are synonyms. Antonyms are words that mean the opposite of one another. *Up* and *down* are antonyms. When you want to know the synonyms or antonyms of a word, use the thesaurus.

Words are divided into categories in the thesaurus. Different categories of words are used to express different kinds of ideas. To find the synonyms of a word in the thesaurus, first turn to the index. Find the word in the index. It is organized alphabetically. Beneath the word you will find its synonyms, listed in order by category numbers.

Here is a partial index from *Roget's International Thesaurus*, p. 1059. (Copyright 1977 by Harper & Row, Publishers, Inc. Reprinted by permission of Harper & Row, Publishers, Inc.) Parts have been labeled for you.

The Word—**lodging**

Parts of Speech			
	nouns	abode	191.1
		habitation	188.1
		housing	188.3	Category Numbers
		quarters	191.3
	adjective	resident	188.13

Select the best synonym for your purposes; then look up its category number in the numbered section of the thesaurus. There you'll find all the synonyms and other words often associated with the word. You can use a thesaurus to help you find just the right words to say what is on your mind when you are writing or speaking.

Here are some other ways to say *lodging* from the numbered section of *Roget's International Thesaurus* (1977, pp. 112-113).

188.   Habitation (an inhabiting)

.1 Nouns   **habitation**   inhabiting, inhabitation, inhabitancy, tenancy, occupancy, occupation, residence, or residency, residing, abiding, living in, nesting, dwelling, commorancy, lodging, staying, stopping, sojourning, staying over; squatting; cohabitation; abode **191**.

.3   **housing**   domiciliation; lodgment, lodging, transient lodging, doss [Britt], quartering, billeting, hospitality; living quarters 191.3; functional housing, housing development, subdivision, tract....

191.   Abode, habitation (place of habitation or resort)

.1 Nouns   **abode**   habitation, place, dwelling, dwelling place....residence; domicile, domus [L.]; lodging, lodgment, lodging place; seat, nest, tabernacle [fig.], cantonment; place, address.

You can also use a thesaurus in research. Suppose you are assigned a report which has to do with the topic *lodgings*. If you first make a list of synonyms and related terms, you then can look up all the names your topic may go by to be sure you find the best information. If you look up *lodging* in the encyclopedia and find no information and no cross-reference, don't give up your search. A thesaurus may give you other words for *lodging* that will help you find the information you need.

Using Roget's Thesaurus
   Directions: Answer each of the following in the space provided.
1. How are words organized in the index of the thesaurus?

_____

2. Synonyms are listed for the words in the index.   T   F

3. Lists of synonyms are grouped by part of speech.   T   F
4. What do the category numbers tell you?

_____

5. How many places in the numbered section of the thesaurus have information related to *lodgings*?   _____
6. What is the name of category number 188?

_____

7. What is the name of category number 191?

_____

8. What category number has to do with the adjective forms of the word *lodging*? _____
9. Why are some of the words in boldface print?

_____

The Atlas. An atlas is a book of maps. The name of an atlas often tells the area pictured in its maps. A world atlas, for example, would contain maps of all the countries of the world. A United States atlas would contain maps of all the states, and so on. Information about population, topography, agriculture, industry, and natural resources is often provided with the maps in order to give a more complete description of the area.

Nearly every atlas uses a grid system to help the user quickly locate places of interest on its maps. Here is an example of a grid in which the rows are numbered and the columns are lettered:

	A	B	C	D	E	
1	*					1
2						2
3						3
	A	B	C	D	E	

Find the asterisk in section A1. Column A and Row 1 meet in this section of the grid. The vertical rows and horizontal columns divide the whole rectangular area of the grid into smaller sections. Any section on the grid can be quickly found by first locating the correct lettered column, and then looking across the correct numbered row until you find the section where the correct row and column meet. Can you figure out which of the following sections is at the center of the grid pictured above? Circle the coordinates (column and row) of your answer.

A1   B2   C2   D3   E1

Using an Atlas

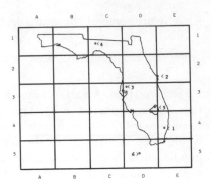

AREA 58,560 sq. mi.
POPULATION 6,789,443
CAPITAL Tallahassee
LARGEST CITY Jacksonville
HIGHEST POINT 345 ft. (Walton County)
SETTLED IN 1565
ADMITTED TO UNION March 3, 1845
POPULAR NAME Sunshine State; Peninsula State
STATE FLOWER Orange Blossom
STATE BIRD Mockingbird

Directions: Write the grid coordinates of each of the following points of interest which have been numbered on the map. The first one is done for you.

1. Miami   __E4__

2. Cape Canaveral   _____

3. Tampa   _____

4. Tallahassee   _____

5. Lake Okeechobee   _____

6. Key West   _____

The almanac. An almanac is an annual or yearly collection of detailed knowledge on a great variety of topics. Almost any important fact which is part of the public record can be found in an almanac. These facts are gathered together and indexed in one volume. This is part of the index of *The World Almanac and Book of Facts*, 1982 edition (copyright © Newspaper Enterprise Association, Inc., 1981, New York 10166):

       Graham and Robinson

This table is from page 131 of the *World Almanac and Book of Facts*, 1982 edition, and has to do with the topic of *Energy Costs*:

Average Consumer Cost of Fuels
Source: Department of Energy (1972 constant dollars)

Fuel	1974	1975	1976	1977	1978	1979	1980
Leaded regular gasoline (cent/gal)	44.8	43.7	43.1	43.2	41.0	49.8	119.1
Residential heating oil (cent/gal)	29.4	29.3	30.2	31.2	31.7	40.8	97.8
Residential natural gas (cent/mcf)	123.4	132.8	145.4	162.2	163.5	185.3	391.5
Residential electricity (cent/kwh)	2.63	7.73	2.77	2.81	2.76	2.66	5.36

mcf = million cubic feet   kwh = million kilowatt hours.

Notice that this table has no information about 1981 or 1982 fuel costs, yet it was published in the 1982 *World Almanac*. This was not an oversight. When using an almanac, keep in mind that a 1982 almanac would have been prepared in 1981, and that the most recent information in 1981 may have been collected in 1980.

Directions: Use the partial index and table from the *World Almanac and Book of Facts 1982* to answer the following questions.
1. How many pages have to do with facts about energy? _____
2. On what page is there information about the measurement of energy? _____
3. Which pages have to do with making energy? _____
4. According to the table of consumer fuel costs, how much did 10 gallons of regular gasoline cost in 1974? _____
   in 1980? _____
5. Which costs more, a gallon of regular gasoline or a gallon of heating oil? _____

6. How much did the cost of electricity increase
   between 1975 and 1976? _____
   between 1979 and 1980? _____

Library Resources

Students who have yet to learn efficient library use procedures
may be overwhelmed by the great variety of print and nonprint
resources of the school or public library. Immature readers at all grade
levels tend to avoid solving study problems at the library, turning
instead to familiar reference resources available at home. Locating
appropriate sources of information is a task which, by nature, is directly
linked to a specific study assignment. Class visits to the library are
occasionally wasted on students who have no immediate study
problems which require library solutions. Direct and systematic
instruction in the use of library resources is most effective and relevant
when conducted within the context of an ongoing study assignment.
Tell your students what kind of information to look for, then show them
how to find it. Successful participation in direct, purposeful library
experiences will provide for a ready transfer of library use skills in
subsequent study situations.

The card catalog. Wouldn't it be nice if someone read every book
in the library, and then organized a system to make it easier for you to
find just the book you want? Actually, the card catalog is just such a
system. Before a book becomes part of a library collection, at least three
index cards are prepared which identify it.

Title card. One kind of card prepared for each book is the title
card; the parts of this title card have been labeled for you:

Title	Fun with American literature
Call Number	
With first letter of author's last name	793.73 Churchill E. Richard
	C Abingdon 1968
Author	Games and puzzles on
Publisher	all phases of American
Date of Publication	literature
Brief Description	254 p.
Number of pages	H.W. Wilson Co., 1968

Graham and Robinson

The title of the book is the first item of information at the top of the title card. When searching the card catalog for the title of this book, you would look under the letter *F* for *Fun*—the first important word in the book's title.

Author card. Another kind of card prepared for each book is the author card. Notice how the arrangement of information on the author card differs from the title card.

Author (last name,	Churchill, E. Richard
first name)	
Title	793.73 Fun with American
	literature
	C Abingdon, 1968
	Games and puzzles on
	all phases of American
	literature.
	254 p.
	H.W. Wilson Co., 1968

The name of the book's author appears at the top of the author card. When searching the card catalog for the author of this book, you would look under the letter *C* for *Churchill*—the first letter of the author's last name.

Subject card. The third kind of card prepared for each book is the subject card. What additional information does a subject card provide?

Subject	Word games
Author	793.73 Churchill, E. Richard
Title	C Fun with American
	literature
	Games and puzzles on
	all phases of American
	literature.
	254 p.
	H.W. Wilson Co., 1968

The topic of the book is the first item of information that appears at the top of the subject card. In all other ways, the subject card is the same as the author card. There may be many different books on the same subject. All books on the same subject are grouped together in the card catalog.

The title, author, and subject cards for each book in the library are stored in a cabinet called the card catalog:

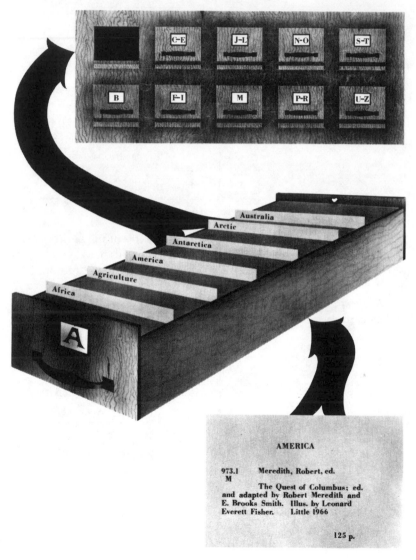

AMERICA

973.1   Meredith, Robert, ed.
M
        The Quest of Columbus; ed.
and adapted by Robert Meredith and
E. Brooks Smith. Illus. by Leonard
Everett Fisher.   Little 1966

                            125 p.

Graham and Robinson

The title, author, and subject cards are arranged in alphabetical order by first important word of the title, author's last name, or first important word of the topic. The drawers of the card catalog are labeled to let you know which part of the alphabet each contains. Some libraries use a separate cabinet for each kind of card (title, author, and subject).

Using the Card Catalog

Directions: Write the letter or letters of the drawer in which you would find cards having to do with each of the titles or authors.

1. *The Pigman* _____
2. Jesse Woodson James _____
3. *The Environment of Man* _____
4. *Jungle Book* _____

5. Rudyard Kipling _____

6. *Above the Civil War* _____
7. Judy Blume _____
8. *Santa Fe Trail* _____
9. *Yankee Doodle Dandy* _____

10. *Pioneers of the Old Southwest* _____

The Dewey Decimal System. Once you find the card of a book you want in the card catalog, how do you find the book itself in the library? Wouldn't it be nice if someone went through all the cards in the card catalog, and labeled them with the exact location of each book on the shelves? The Dewey Decimal System does just that by separating all the nonfiction books in the library into categories and subcategories, depending upon the subject of the book:

Major Classifications of the Dewey Decimal System
(Collier's Encyclopedia, 1974, pp. 591-592)

Number	Category	Representative Titles	
000-099	General Works		
010	Bibliography	*The Research Handbook*	001.4
020	Library science	*Libraries and You*	028.7
030	Encyclopedias	*Collier's Encyclopedia*	031
040	Collected essays	*Get That Story*	070.69
050	Periodicals	*The Best of the Smithsonian*	081
060	Societies		
070	Newspapers		
080	Collected works		
090	Manuscripts and rare books		

Number	Category	Representative Titles	
100-199	Philosophy		
110	Metaphysics	*The Mysteries of Reincarnation*	129.4
120	Metaphysical theories	*ESP*	133.8
130	Psychology (branches)	*Psychology in Action*	150
140	Philosophy	*To Teens With Love*	170.202
150	Psychology	*Yoga for Physical and Mental Fitness*	181.45
160	Logic		
170	Ethics		
180	Ancient and Medieval		
190	Philosophy (Modern)		

Number	Category	Representative Titles	
200-299	Religion		
210	Natural theology	*Religions East and West*	200.9
220	Bible	*Bible Times*	220.9
230	Doctrinal theology	*Jesus of Nazareth*	232.9
240	Devotional & practical	*Prayers and Graces of Thanksgiving*	264.1
250	Pastoral theology	*World's Great Religions*	290
260	Christian church	*Greek Myths*	292
270	Christian church (history)		
280	Christian churches and sects		
290	Other religions		

Number	Category	Representative Titles	
300-399	Social Sciences		
310	Statistics	*Riot 1*	301.18
320	Political Science	*Africa Independent*	320.9
330	Economics	*Economic Development*	330.9
340	Law	*Your Legal Rights as a Minor*	340
350	Public administration	*How Our Government Began*	350
360	Social welfare	*The Right to Bear Arms*	363.3
370	Education	*Transportation of Tomorrow*	380.5
380	Public services	*Folklore in America*	378
390	Customs and folklore		

Number	Category	Representative Titles	
400-499	Language		
410	Comparative Linguistics	*Man Must Speak*	410
420	English & Anglo Saxon	*Words*	422
430	Germanic Languages		
440	French	*Modern Complete French Grammar*	448.242
450	Italian, Rumanian		
460	Spanish, Portuguese	*A Trip to Mexico*	468.3
470	Latin		
480	Greek		
490	Other languages	*Chinese Writing*	495.1

Graham and Robinson

500-599	Pure science		
510	Mathematics	*Mathematics for the Modern Mind*	510
520	Astronomy	*Discover the Stars*	520
530	Physics	*Understanding Physics*	530
540	Chemistry		
550	Earth sciences	*Deep Sea World*	551.4
560	Paleontology	*Prehistoric World*	560
570	Anthropology & Biology		
580	Botany		
590	Zoology	*Monsters of the Deep*	591.92

600-699	Technology		
610	Medicine	*The Dawn of Medicine*	610.9
620	Engineering	*Engineering in History*	620.9
630	Agriculture		
640	Home economics	*Art of Homemaking*	640
650	Business	*Silk Screen Techniques*	655.3
660	Chemical technology		
670	Manufactures		
680	Other manufactures	*Country Furniture*	684.1
690	Building construction		

700-799	The Arts		
710	Landscape		
720	Architecture		
730	Sculpture		
740	Drawing	*Pioneer Art in America*	745
750	Painting	*Collage*	751
760	Prints		
770	Photography	*My Hobby is Photography*	770
780	Music	*Musical Instruments of Africa*	781
790	Recreation	*Complete Book of Games and Stunts*	790

800-899	Literature		
810	American	*Poems for Youth*	811.08
820	English	*An Introduction to Shakespeare*	822.3
830	German		
840	French	*French Poetry*	841.08
850	Italian, Rumanian	*Dante's Inferno*	851
860	Spanish, Portuguese		
870	Latin		
880	Greek		
890	Other languages	*African Voices*	896

900-999	History		
910	Geography	*Lost Cities and Vanished Civilizations*	913
920	Biography	*Benjamin Franklin*	921
930	Ancient history	*The Near East*	939
940	Europe		
950	Asia	*India*	954
960	Africa	*The Blue Nile*	960
970	North America		
980	South America		
990	Other parts of the world		

Many different numbers are used to separate the different topics in each Dewey Decimal System category. Only books about the same topic have the same Dewey Decimal number. The Dewey Decimal number is printed on each book so that it can be seen when the book is shelved. The same number (known as the *call number*) is printed on each of the catalog cards for the book. Because the cards, shelves, and books are all numbered according to the Dewey Decimal System, you can quickly find any nonfiction book you want.

Fiction books are separated from nonfiction books in the library. Fiction books are shelved and called for alphabetically, by author's last name. Some books may be used only within the library itself, you can't sign them out. These books are reference books, and a capital *R* is often printed under their call number to let you know. Books for children, or juveniles, often have a capital *J* printed on them. If a book is kept in a separate section of the library, chances are that there will be a letter code with the call number to let you know where.

Providing Practice in Using the Dewey Decimal System

School librarian Martha Murphy helps students discover the organization of the Dewey Decimal System by involving them in a clever "treasure hunt" activity. Following the traditional explanation of how the library works, Mrs. Murphy distributes a floor plan which represents each bookcase as an empty box. The students are instructed to fill each box with the Dewey Decimal number of the first book in the appropriate bookcase (including appropriate letters for fiction, biography, nonfiction, and special collections). Students are asked to select one interesting title for each of the ten major classifications of the Dewey Decimal System, and two from fiction while they complete their "treasure hunt." When they have finished, the students compare their answers by filling in Mrs. Murphy's chalkboard floor plan together. The floor plan bookcases are then grouped and labeled according to the major classifications of the Dewey Decimal System. After a question and answer session, students are invited to borrow any of the books they found interesting during their search.

Graham and Robinson

The Library of Congress System. Some libraries are organized according to the Library of Congress System, instead of the Dewey Decimal system. This is the classification system used in the greatest of American libraries, The Library of Congress, in Washington D.C. Letters, rather than numbers, separate the major classifications (*Collier's Encyclopedia*, 1974, p. 591):

A   General Works—Polygraphy
B   Philosophy—Religion
C   History Auxiliary Sciences
D   History and Topography (except America)
E-F America
G   Geography—Anthropology
H   Social Sciences
J   Political Science
K   Law
L   Education
M   Music
N   Fine Arts
P   Language and Literature
Q   Science
R   Medicine
S   Agriculture
T   Technology
U   Military Science
V   Naval Science
Z   Bibliography and Library Science

A number is provided following the major classification letter for each book. The number helps to identify the specific topic of the book, as in the Dewey Decimal System. The Library of Congress system and the Dewey Decimal System both help library users quickly locate the books they need.

The Readers' Guide to Periodical Literature. Not all of the information in the library is contained in books. A great deal of information is published in newspapers, magazines, and other periodicals. Wouldn't it be nice if someone read all of the most popular magazines, and then organized a guide book to help you quickly find any article by author or subject? Actually, the *Readers' Guide to Periodical Literature* is just such a reference book.

Here is a sample entry from the May 1982 issue of the *Readers' Guide to Periodical Literature* (p. 119):

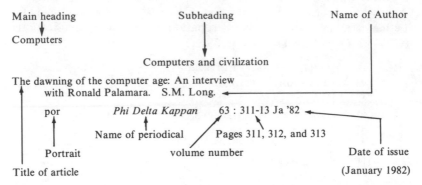

This entry means that S.M. Long wrote a three page article about computers and civilization for the January 1982 issue of *Phi Delta Kappan* magazine. The title of the article was "The dawning of the computer age: An interview with Ronald Palamara," and included a portrait.

Over 150 periodicals are indexed in the *Readers' Guide.* There is also an *Abridged Readers' Guide* which indexes about 40 periodicals (for smaller libraries). Collections of monthly issues of the *Readers' Guide* are bound in annual volumes.

Other library resources. Students should visit the library regularly to become familiar with the variety of materials and services provided there. Many students are unaware that most libraries offer much more than books. They should be encouraged to discover first hand the variety of resources available to the public in many libraries.

- media centers (supplied with audiovisual equipment and materials, sound recordings, TV)

- microform (newspapers, magazines, and other material on microfilm and microfiche)

- special collections (large print and talking books for the visually handicapped, picture file, vertical file)

- community centers (guest speakers, seminars, club and organization meetings)

- exhibits (arts and crafts, cultural awareness)
- entertainment (performances and recitals by local artists, motion pictures)

Anticipating the Writer's Message

The effectiveness of the entire study process should be viewed in terms of the gain in new information and ideas which results from completing study assignments. How much students may gain as a result of their efforts may be determined by comparing what they already know to what they are presently learning. Writers direct the flow of information and ideas within a given selection in ways which they feel will take learners from where they are at the outset to a point of higher achievement.

Students need to be shown how to use what they already know to anticipate the writer's message in whatever form it is communicated. Each of the textbook reader aids, reference resources, and library resources discussed earlier in this chapter is organized according to a generally accepted and easily recognizable format. Strategies for locating the information in an encyclopedia, for example, are pretty much the same for all encyclopedias. For the great majority of written discourse, however, one set of strategies will not cover all the techniques which writers may use to get a message across. Getting in "synch" with a variety of individual writers, and reasoning within their various writing styles, demands a high level of linguistic knowledge and flexibility. Communication suffers if the reader's skills are much less developed than the writer's.

Reading should be an active, dynamic process of interaction between reader and author. Unfortunately, many students become passive, teacher-dependent learners simply because they are given help they don't really need in order to solve their study problems. Active, independent learners take risks, make "educated" guesses, explore alternatives, occasionally disagree, yet are willing to entertain disagreeable views until they can be proved or disproved. Passive learners wait to be told what to do, avoid taking chances or guessing, and generally look to someone else to solve their problems.

The kinds of questions you ask, and the kinds of answers you value will encourage or discourage independent thinking. Don't allow students to passively follow the writer's thoughts; encourage independent thinking at every opportunity. Anticipating the writer's message before the eyes meet the page of print helps foster habits of active learning.

Teacher-directed techniques for helping students organize their experience in anticipation of the writer's message are called preorganizers. Teachers may (and should) use preorganizers with students of all grade levels. Preorganizers are structured to help ensure that learners regard reading as an active information gathering process. And since preorganizers involve students in purpose setting, they simulate what students should do independently as mature readers.

Research on various types of preorganizers shows mixed results in terms of comprehension improvement. It seems obvious that preorganizers are not useful, and can even interfere with comprehension, if students possess organized preknowledge to bring to a given reading experience. When material is difficult, new, or poorly organized, however, it seems equally obvious that a preorganizer should be helpful. The preorganizers described in the section which follows have all been successful with groups of students in a variety of situations.

Advance Organizer

Ausubel (1968) is credited with first coining the term *advance organizer* for what has grown to be a family of related preorganizing techniques. There are several variations on Ausubel's basic theme, but each is rooted in the principal that learners can benefit from a general introduction to the topic of a longer reading selection.

Ausubel's advance organizer is a brief reading passage, usually a paragraph or so in length. The high level of generality of the passage can provide a "least common denominator" to which students may relate their previous experience with the topic. Directing the students' attention to the higher to lower level of generality expressed in the relationship between the advance organizer and the longer reading selection seems to capture their interest while:

1. building anticipation and predictive reading skills;
2. helping students relate their previous experiences to the printed words; and
3. establishing general purposes for reading.

Some teachers write their own advance organizer passages, while others "borrow" them from reference sources.

This advance organizer was used in an earth science class, preceding a longer reading selection on cyclone formation (Blanc, Fischler, & Gardner, 1967, p. 145):

Whenever there is a difference in temperature between two bodies of air, convection currents are set up. The warm air expands, becomes less dense, and rises. The cooler, denser neighboring air pushes down under the warmer air. The winds are deflected, or change course, because the earth's rotation on its axis.

Structured Overview

Another type of organizer is the structured overview reported by Earle (1969). The structured overview is a readiness technique in which key terms in a selection to be read are arranged in diagram form. The structured overview is designed to illustrate important relationships as a semantic (meaning) organizer.

During the course of a unit on the organization of living things, a life science class had dissected a frog. The teacher made a list of the important words from that experience and wrote them on the chalkboard. The structured overview that follows was constructed using the word list from the board and new words from the chapter to be read on multicellular animals as organisms:

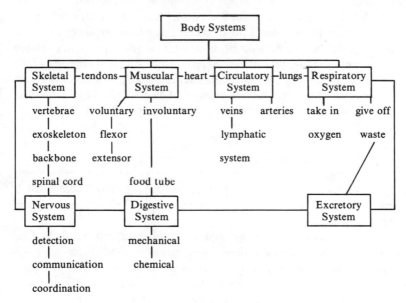

The structured overview was discussed in depth. The teacher answered the students' questions, elaborated on the important relationships, and then the chapter was read.

To make a structured overview, first review the reading selection and make a list of key vocabulary words and important terms. Organize the list into diagram form by trial and error, until an arrangement is found which illustrates:

1. the hierarchy of major concepts;
2. the connections between the concepts as presented in the selection to be read; and
3. the comparison pattern expressed implicitly in the structured overview.

Semantic Organizer

A semantic organizer is a map or diagram developed after brainstorming about a topic to be read. It helps students organize broad concepts and the relationships between them. It may also serve as a postorganizer as exemplified here.

A health class was about to read a chapter on nutrition. One of the key concepts to be developed was the importance of a balanced diet. The teacher initiated a discussion by asking some questions:

What are the food groups necessary for good nutrition?

Do you know what I mean when I say food groups?

The teacher wrote a list of the key terms and vocabulary related to food groups as the students answered the questions. At the end of the discussion, the class had developed an acceptable definition of the term *food groups*. Then the teacher organized the list of key terms and vocabulary into structured overview form on the chalkboard:

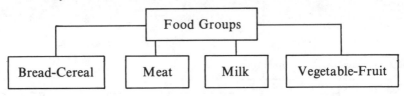

The teacher then suggested that the students read to find examples of how each of these food groups contributes to good nutrition and a balanced diet. The structured overview was then transferred to a ditto. Several empty boxes were added, and a copy was distributed to each student. Next, they were asked to fill in three ways that each food group contributes to good nutrition and a balanced diet.

Graham and Robinson

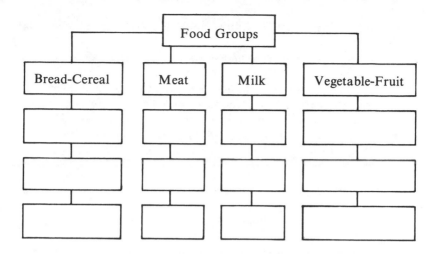

After the chapter was read and students had written their responses, the teacher again initiated a discussion. Students shared their responses and discussed why some found less and others more than three examples for each food group. This activity provided the teacher with verification that the concept had been developed, and the students with closure on the topic.

Purpose Questions

Establishing specific purposes for reading can be accomplished through questioning. Purpose questions should guide students toward essential information and ideas. They should also help capture the students' interest—an important ingredient for improving comprehension. Try to ask questions which will build anticipation of both important and interesting content, and be sure that your questions are answered in the text of the selection. Students need specific purposes for reading before they can actively and efficiently reach for an understanding of the writer's work.

One method of generating purpose questions is to select and adapt textbook guide and review questions. Here are some general guidelines for generating purpose questions (categories from Thomas & Robinson, 1982, pp. 62-66) coupled with examples of selected and adapted guide and review questions from a social studies textbook (Schwartz & O'Connor, 1971).

1. Broad purpose questions require more than reading for superficial details.

   What are the strengths and weaknesses of the U.N. as a peace keeping organization?

   > Minor questions may be asked in order to help the students find the facts they will need to make inferences or draw conclusions demanded by broad purpose questions.

   What were five achievements of the U.N. during its first twenty years? What are three serious problems of the U.N. today?

2. Try to design questions which will capture the students' interest.

   A group of ten people enters and settles in Zinch Valley. Write an essay answering the following questions:
   1. *What are the immediate and long range problems these people face?*
   2. *What are the solutions these people bring to bear on both the immediate and the long range problems?*

That's all. No other information is provided.

   But in class there will be an opportunity for questions. For the last thirty minutes of that period, and those thirty minutes only, students may ask questions. They may have *all* the information they can pull out of their teacher in thirty minutes.

3. Colorful phrasing may generate imaginative speculations.

   During President Truman's reelection campaign he toured the country telling crowds of people about the "do-nothing, good-for-nothing 80th Congress." What was he talking about? Why would he say such things to the American public?

4. Purpose questions can help students prepare for a demanding or challenging task.

   Judging by what happened during the 1920s and 1930s, can a great nation like the United States isolate itself in the modern world?

   Use the information in Chapter 14 to prepare for a debate in which you will give reasons why the United States can't stay isolated. I will defend the opposite position.

5. Conflicting evidence can put the students in the middle of a "hot" issue when decisions must be made.

   Suppose you were a Senator from Virginia in 1860. After Lincoln's election you are approached by other Southerners to join the

Confederate States of America. What would your reasons be for and against joining such a movement?

6. Personalized questions can drive the author's message home.
   President Roosevelt promised the American people and their allies four freedoms early in World War II: Freedom of speech, freedom of worship, freedom from want, and freedom from fear. How did people lose these freedoms during World War II? Would you fight to keep these freedoms today? Why or why not?

7. Purpose questions can put students into the shoes of others.
   Theodore Roosevelt played many roles during his career: cowboy, historian, police commissioner, Naval Secretary, Rough Rider, Governor of New York State, Vice President, President, peacemaker, and hunter. Which role do you think he liked the best?

8. Purpose questions can transport students through space and time as they acquire vicarious experiences.
   How would you compare a typical day in the life of a millionaire such as John D. Rockefeller in the early 1900s with that of a sweatshop worker at the same time in history?

Teachers so often take responsibility for generating purpose questions for their students that many students never really learn how to create purpose questions for themselves. Other prereading questioning techniques presented in this section involve learners in creating purpose questions with their teachers and on their own.

ReQuest

ReQuest (Manzo, 1969, pp. 123-126, 163) is a technique which involves teachers and students in a kind of structured question and answer game. The game begins with all the players (teacher and students) reading the first sentence of the selection together. The teacher's book is then closed, and the students are free to ask the teacher questions about the first sentence. After answering, the teacher may make recommendations to the students for the improvement of their questions. Students should be encouraged to ask questions which build anticipation and establish purposes for reading the remainder of the selection. Next, the students close their books and the teacher poses model questions for them to answer. The procedure is continued throughout the first paragraph or so, until the students actively speculate as to the nature of the content of the selection. Teachers may prefer to select key sentences from throughout the selection rather than limiting the technique to beginning sentences exclusively.

An English class used the ReQuest technique with one of the selections from their literature text (Safir, 1980, p. 99):

"War" by Jack London

First Sentence
"He was a young man, not more than twenty-four or -five, and he might have sat his horse with the careless grace of his youth had be not been so catlike and tense."

Anthony's Question
Why was the young man so catlike and tense?
Teacher's Answer
The young man is a soldier on patrol in time of war. He must be alert to attack the enemy and to defend himself.
Suzanne's Question
What does "he might have sat his horse with the careless grace of his youth" mean?
Teacher's Answer
At the time this young man lived, people his age would usually ride their horses for pleasure.
Tom's Question
When does this story take place?
Teacher's Answer
The information in this story leads me to believe that it probably takes place during the Civil War, although the author never really says so.

Second Sentence
"His black eyes roved everywhere, catching the movements of twigs and branches where small birds hopped, questing ever onward through the changing vistas of trees and brush, and returning always to the clumps of undergrowth on either side."

Teacher's Question
Why do you suppose the soldier's eyes always return to the undergrowth?
Michael's Answer
Maybe he was separated from the other soldiers and now he's looking for them.
Therese's Answer
He may think that someone is hiding there to kill him.
Kathy's Answer
Since this soldier notices every small detail and never seems to relax, I think he doesn't know where the enemy soldiers are. He's probably in a really dangerous area for him.

Students who apply this technique on their own engage in what is termed "creative reading." Creative reading refers to the process of active questioning and speculation conducted by the learner throughout the text. With teacher direction, or on their own, students should learn to read purposefully. Answering questions and/or confirming or rejecting speculations made prior to reading helps ensure that students read for meaning throughout each assignment.

PReP

PReP (Langer, 1981) is a mnemonic for Judith A. Langer's prereading plan. This three step readiness technique makes use of questioning and discussion before reading for both assessment and instruction. The instructional procedure is straightforward, yet effective *if* (as Langer cautions) the teacher understands *why* it works. Langer explains that "...we can help students comprehend a text by creating conditions under which appropriate knowledge is brought to awareness and applied. This permits a link between text concepts and past experiences and sets up, in the mind of the learner, appropriate expectations about the language and content of the text."

Here's how PReP works.

Phase 1. *Initial associations with the concept to be developed in the text.* The teacher asks each student to tell anything that comes to mind when a certain key term is mentioned. The term selected should be central to an understanding of the selection to be read. The students' responses to this "word association test" will reveal their level of prior knowledge about the topic. Keep group size small (10 or less seems best) so you can really listen to each student's response. Decide if the student has *much* prior knowledge (when the response is a definition, synonym, or analogy, for example); *some* prior knowledge (when the response is an example or characteristic); or *little* prior knowledge (when the response does not reveal much of the substance or character of what the term represents). Once you have determined the level of prior knowledge each student has to bring to the printed page, you are ready for the next phase of the plan.

Phase 2. *Reflections on initial associations.* The teacher should initiate and guide a discussion around the question, "What made you think of your response?" Each student should be encouraged to participate in the discussion and gain insight from the other members of the group.

Phase 3. *Reformulation of knowledge.* Encourage the students to verbalize any information or ideas gained through the class discussion. In this phase of the plan the teacher should say to the students, "Based on our discussion and before we read the text, have you any new ideas about the key term?"

This activity gives the teacher a window through which to view how individual students acquire and organize knowledge in anticipation of reading. Following through on each phase of Langer's prereading plan not only helps prepare learners for reading assignments, but also helps teachers prepare appropriate reading assignments.

Expanding Understanding through Multilevel Questioning

The kinds of questions teachers ask greatly influence the kinds of answers their students give. One way teachers can help students develop a dimension of depth in their understanding of the meanings and significance of printed words is by posing a variety of questions to them. The lowest level of understanding involves recognition and recall— locating and relating small pieces of factual information. Here is an example of such a question for Poe's "The Cask of Amontillado." *What did Fortunato do to Montresor in the first paragraph of the story?*

The next highest level of comprehension involves the making of inferences and the application of logic in the absence of specific information. This kind of question requires a greater contribution on the part of the learner than merely locating or recognizing directly stated information. *How does Montresor go about getting his revenge?*

A third level of understanding involves the learner in critically analyzing facts and inferences. This type of critical comprehension question requires the comparison of information and ideas presented by the writer with those already held by the reader. *Why does Fortunato insist upon tasting the Amontillado?*

The highest level of comprehension involves the reader in raising new questions and gaining new insights about information and ideas represented in print. This level of understanding requires the greatest contribution on the part of the learner. Let's call questions of this kind *creative* comprehension questions—the kind that ask learners to utilize new information in original ways. *How could the situation involving Fortunato and Montresor be used as an example to help avert a potentially destructive situation in real life?*

Teachers can help learners gain a measure of depth in their understanding through the use of pre and postreading questioning techniques. Keep in mind that the overall goal of teaching study skills is to develop independent learners. A steady diet of the teacher's questions does not necessarily help students achieve independence. How can teachers help students make the transition from teacher-dependence to independence? Are there no intermediate teacher-directed techniques which make use of the principles of effective questioning?

One way to shift a greater measure of responsibility for learning to students is to prepare and distribute structured-response activities or guides. Two excellent sources on the preparation and use of guides in the teaching of reading and study skills are Herber's *Teaching Reading in Content Areas* (1978) and Robinson's *Teaching Reading, Writing and Study Strategies: The Content Areas* (1983). The specific format of guides presented in this section are adapted from another fine source book, *Reading and Learning in the Content Classroom,* by Estes and Vaughan, (1978, pp. 156-176).

Study Guide

Study guides use questions to develop the readers' skills at reasoning within and beyond the text. The teacher designs the guide around four levels of comprehension. The students select appropriate answers to questions written on various levels of comprehension.

Here's a study guide distributed for use by an English class.

Study Guide for the Short Story, "The Cask of Amontillado"

What did the author say? (check two)
_____ a. Montresor must not only punish, but punish with impunity.
_____ b. Fortunato is a nice person.
_____ c. The taste of wine was worth the trip.
_____ d. Montresor was a mason.

What did the author mean? (check two)
_____ a. Fortunato and Montresor were good friends.
_____ b. Montresor had an elaborate plan to kill Fortunato.
_____ c. Montresor intended to wall Fortunato into a niche.
_____ d. Nitre spoils the taste of wine.

Of what significance is the author's meaning? (check two)
_____ a. Montresor is insane.
_____ b. Fortunato is a hero.
_____ c. Montresor's plan is fool-proof.
_____ d. Fortunato is a martyr.

How can we use the meaning? (check two)
_____ a. Don't give people cause to want revenge against you.
_____ b. Don't allow yourself to be manipulated by flattery.
_____ c. Stay out of basements.
_____ d. Don't drink wine.

Secondary students who can complete this guide on their own are one step closer to independence in reasoning within and beyond the text. The guide simulates the kind of questioning activity ordinarily conducted by the teacher to expand understanding. Students should be weaned from guides once they have learned to ask and answer questions to gain a greater measure of depth in understanding on their own. Study guides are equally useful for elementary students, provided that they are ready to take this transitional step toward independent learning.

Concept Guide

Concept guides can be prepared to help students simulate semantic organizer activities ordinarily conducted by the teacher. This concept guide was prepared for use by a science class learning about the microscope.

The Microscope: An Aid to Observation
(Brandwein & others, 1975, pp. 472-474)

Part I.
As you read about the microscope, fill in the blanks in the statements with the appropriate part of the microscope from the word list below:

1. The microscope is mounted on a weighted _____ that gives it stability.
2. The ocular lens system is also called the _____.
3. Carry the microscope with one hand on the _____ and the other under the base.
4. The eyepiece fits into the _____.
5. The _____ fits into the eyepiece, offering a variety of magnifications.
6. Pressure applied to the side of one of the objectives will cuase the _____ to revolve.
7. The two adjustments used to focus the microscope are the _____ and the _____.
8. The slide is placed on the _____.
9. The flexible _____ hold the slide in place.
10. The _____ reflects the light through the hole in the stage, which is controlled by the _____.

clips	nosepiece	mirror
objective lenses	stage	arm
coarse adjustment	tube	base
fine adjustment	eyepiece	diaphragm

Part II.
Group each of the parts of the microscope from the word list above under the appropriate category below:

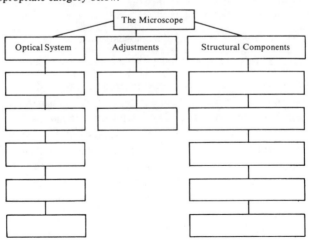

Graham and Robinson

Any number of different kinds of guides can be prepared to simulate the different kinds of activities teachers ordinarily conduct with their students. Teachers should monitor their students' progress and help them internalize the purpose(s) of the guides. When they are ready to guide their own reading and study, your students will still need support, encouragement, and advice in refining and coordinating their skills (feedback). Individual guidance is most effective when provided as problems arise. The best time to be available to help individual students refine and coordinate their study skills is while their eyes are on the page of print, which is the topic of our next chapter.

Reaction Guide

Part I. What did the writer say? (check four)

_____ Building a sufficient body of prestudy experience, and organizing this experience in anticipation of a specific study task, can help learners find the meaning of the printed words they read.

_____ Textbook reader aids make print less complex for readers.

_____ Many reader aids are organized in alphabetic or numeric sequence.

_____ Teachers can assume that most students have reference resources in their homes and know how to use them.

_____ Review questions presented at the conclusion of a segment of text should actually be read in advance.

_____ Students should be given library assignments on a regular basis, especially book reports.

_____ Learners can benefit from a general introduction to the topic of a longer reading selection.

_____ Questioning activities force readers to do their best work.

_____ Study guides should be provided for all students engaged in reading content area material.

Part II. What did the writer mean? (check four)

_____ Students wouldn't need teachers if they knew how to use reader aids.

_____ Questioning activities can either build anticipation and enrich understanding, or provide busy work and discourage thinking depending upon how they are conducted.

_____ Preorganizers ruin the fun of reading by eliminating many of the surprises.

_____ Some problems readers have while their eyes are on the page can be avoided before their eyes meet the page.

_____ The content of the reading material should determine the process the reader uses to gain its meaning.

_____ Independent leaners organize their own study activities effectively.

_____ Primary grade teachers shouldn't need to use study guides.

_____ Secondary grade teachers can assume students know how to use reader aids independently.

Part III. How can we use the meaning?

1. Rich Northridge is a primary grade teacher. He has separated his class into three different ability-level groups for reading instruction. How can he provide for three different levels of reading ability when he teaches the whole class subjects like science and social studies together?

_____

_____

_____

2. Bob Samoville teaches honors Spanish at the junior high school level. He wants his students to research Hispanic culture and prepare a written report on its influence upon their choice of one Central or South American country. What do Mr. Samoville's students need to know in order to complete such an assignment? How can he help ensure their success before they begin?

_____

_____

_____

Graham and Robinson

3. Arleen Leeds has chosen a novel for her high school English class which has no pictures or reader aids. She knows that some of the students may run into difficulty completing the home reading assignments she has planned. What can she do in class to help these students read effectively at home?

_____

_____

_____

These are the answers to the Reaction Guide:

Part I	Part II	Part III
√	___	Answers will vary
___	√	
√	___	
___	√	
√	√	
___	√	
√	___	
___	___	
___	___	

Answers to Pre- and Postreading Activities
Here is how one group of teachers completed the structured overview.

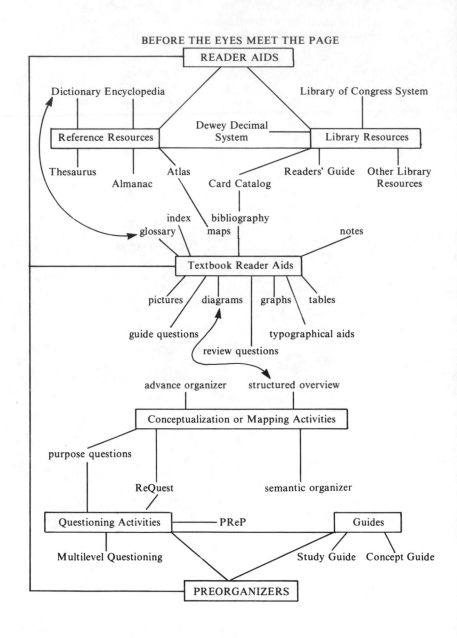

BEFORE THE EYES MEET THE PAGE

READER AIDS

Dictionary Encyclopedia

Library of Congress System

Reference Resources

Dewey Decimal System

Library Resources

Thesaurus

Almanac

Atlas

Card Catalog

Readers' Guide

Other Library Resources

index

bibliography

glossary

maps

notes

Textbook Reader Aids

pictures

diagrams

graphs

tables

guide questions

typographical aids

review questions

advance organizer

structured overview

Conceptualization or Mapping Activities

purpose questions

ReQuest

semantic organizer

Questioning Activities

PReP

Guides

Multilevel Questioning

Study Guide   Concept Guide

PREORGANIZERS

Chapter 3
WHILE THE EYES ARE ON THE PAGE

Study Guide

Place a check mark before each correct statement as you read Chapter Three. Familiarize yourself with this guide and skim the chapter before you begin reading.*

I. *What did the writers say?* (check three)

    _____ a. Some students' problems in processing print are occasionally overlooked and attributed to creative, divergent thinking.

    _____ b. Failure to make inferences based upon information supplied in the text is one way students signal for help in developing flexible language processing strategies.

    _____ c. The ability to answer a variety of questions after reading is the only real proof that students have processed text effectively.

    _____ d. The fear of making mistakes can interfere with fluency and comprehension.

    _____ e. Students will automatically add new strategies in response to new demands upon their language processing skills.

II. *What did the writers mean?* (check three)

    _____ a. Failure to monitor language processing strategies may interfere with the acquisition of more powerful and efficient strategies.

    _____ b. Students need to be shown how to learn from their mistakes.

*Correct answers appear at end of Chapter Three.

_____ c. A particular writer's style and choice of vocabulary should not prohibit a teacher from selecting a text for class use.

_____ d. Some students try to use experience, common knowledge, and common sense to answer their teachers' questions, in order to avoid searching for information in print.

_____ e. Systematic study of basic linguistic structures is a must for all students.

III. *How can we use the meaning?* (check three)

_____ a. Provide students with familiar kinds of written material until they enter high school.

_____ b. Encourage students to take "educated" guesses when they experience uncertainty while reading.

_____ c. Differentiate assignments so that students who avoid processing print are required to answer text based questions.

_____ d. Make students aware of how they go about completing assignments, and how efficient readers would complete similar assignments.

_____ e. Make sure that students read at one steady rate, and that they don't speed up, slow down, or look back unless absolutely necessary.

Once purposes have been set and the meaning search is underway, readers are on their own to discover the key information and ideas represented in the writer's work. Teachers can help ensure that their students' search for meaning will be successful by showing them how to process text strategically. Students must develop and use deliberate strategies for getting the writer's message within, between, and among sentences across a broad spectrum of topics, literary forms, and kinds of discourse.

Questions and Answers

Q. What are the reading strategies of effective readers?

A. Brown ("Metacognitive Development and Reading," *Theoretical Issues in Reading Comprehension*, 1980, p. 456. Copyright 1980 by Lawrence Erlbaum Associates, Inc. Reprinted by permission.) suggests that under the heading, "reading strategies," we incorporate any deliberate planful control of activities that give birth to comprehension. These activities include:

1. clarifying the purposes of reading, that is, understanding the task demands, both explicit and implicit;
2. identifying the aspects of a message that are important;
3. allocating attention so that concentration can be focused on the major content area rather than trivia;
4. monitoring ongoing activities to determine whether comprehension is occurring;
5. engaging in review and self-interrogation to determine whether goals are being achieved;
6. taking corrective action when failures in comprehension are detected; and
7. recovering from disruptions and distractions—and many deliberate, planful activities that render reading an efficient information gathering activity.

In short, the effective reader engages in a variety of deliberate tactics to ensure efficiency. Note that such efficiency involves cognitive economy as well as expenditure of effort. The efficient reader learns to evaluate strategy selection not only in terms of final outcome but in terms of the payoff value of the attempt; information is analyzed only to the depth necessary to meet current needs. This ability implicates a subtle monitoring of the task demands, the reader's own capacities and limitations, and the interaction between the two. All these activities involve *metacognition*, conscious deliberate attempts to understand and orchestrate one's own efforts at being strategic.

Q. What happens when students fail to comprehend?
A. Anderson ("Study Strategies and Adjunct Aids," *Theoretical Issues in Reading Comprehension*, 1980, pp. 498-499. Copyright 1980 by Lawrence Erlbaum Associates, Inc. Reprinted by permission.) presents these conditional answers about what students may do when they fail to comprehend:

1. If readers read something they do not understand, they may decide to take some strategic action immediately or may store the information in memory as a pending question.
2. If readers store the information as pending questions, they may formulate a possible meaning (usually one) that is stored as a tentative hypothesis.

3. If readers form pending questions, they usually continue to read.
4. If a triggering event occurs after the reader forms the pending question (i.e., too many pending questions or repetitions of the same pending question), the reader may take some strategic action.
5. If readers take some strategic action, they may:
   a. *reread* some portion of the text in order to collect more information that will either answer a pending question or form a tentative hypothesis that is related to a pending question;
   b. *jump ahead* in the text to see if there are headings or paragraphs that refer to the pending question and that might answer the pending question;
   c. *consult* an outside source (dictionary, glossary, encyclopedia, expert) for an answer to some pending question;
   d. make a *written record* of a pending question;
   e. *think/reflect* about the pending question and related information that the reader has in memory;
   f. *quit* reading the text.
6. If the strategic action is successful, the reader usually continues to read from the point at which the comprehension failure was last encountered.
7. If the strategic action is not successful the reader usually continues to read by taking some other strategic action.

Q. Suppose comprehension failure shows up only after the student has finished reading. What kinds of help can the teacher provide then?
A. Students who wait until after they have finished reading to find out whether they understand are obviously not monitoring (and perhaps not even aware of) their own reading strategies. Students should be clear about what they know at the outset, and about what they need to know moment to moment throughout the evolving base of information and events. Teachers can help students develop an awareness of the reasons for their failure to comprehend. Teachers can also show students how to develop and regulate their own reading strategies in order to recognize and head-off comprehension failure.

Graham and Robinson

Developing Comprehending Strategies

Every teacher, and every student, has a "theory" of what the reading process is all about. Very often, the best first step toward developing effective reading strategies is to discuss *why* the learner engages in inefficient or unproductive activities. Make time to talk with students who demonstrate difficulty in comprehending *while* their eyes are on the page. Help them substitute more productive strategies when you note the following problems:

- overreliance on prior knowledge
- overreliance on text
- failure to make text based inferences
- overreliance on one set of strategies

Find out why your students act as they do—not only about their attitudes toward reading but, also, about their personal theories of the reading process.

Three Views of the Reading Process

What is your view of the reading process? Are you aware of your students' views? Here are views of three theorists:

Goodman (1976, p. 479) has characterized reading as a "psycholinguistic guessing game," because of his belief that "reading, like listening, is a sampling, predicting, guessing process."

Gough (1976, p. 532) suggests that "the reader is not a guesser. From the outside, (s)he appears to go from print to meaning as if by magic. But...this is an illusion [as]...(s)he really plods through the sentence letter by letter, word by word."

Rumelhart's interactive theory of reading (1977) combines elements of other models, as explained by Wildman and Kling (1978-1979, p. 160): "Plodding through the text letter-by-letter may and will occur to the extent that anticipatory strategies fail. The presence of anticipation can enhance the reading process, but its absence does not preclude it."

Overreliance on Prior Knowledge

One group of students makes use of world knowledge and their ability to make broader context inferences to avoid processing printed information. These students often bring a wealth of knowledge to class discussions, but have problems answering specific questions and avoid making text based inferences. Because they frequently volunteer more information than they are asked for, their problems in processing print are occasionally overlooked and attributed to creative, divergent thinking. Creative thinking should be encouraged, but not as a means to avoid gaining new information and ideas from print.

Differentiating assignments. One way to help ensure that creative thinkers will also learn to be creative readers is to differentiate assignments. Once you have decided to assign a certain group of questions (or activities), take another moment to decide which students would benefit most from taking responsibility for answering specific questions. All students may be assigned all questions, but be selective when deciding who will answer in class. Give text bound learners creative questions to answer. Give students who avoid processing print, text based questions to answer. Try to help your students strike a balance which will afford them a measure of flexibility in completing challenging reading study tasks.

Overreliance on Text

There are many hardworking students who are unwilling to read beyond ambiguous information or an unknown word until they have had their questions answered by a reference source (dictionary, encyclopedia) or expert (teacher, parent). These students fear making mistakes to such an extent that they may not hazard a guess or hold a question in mind—even if it means that more important information may be compromised in the process.

Smith (1971, p. 230), in his psycholinguistic analysis of reading and learning to read, said that

> fluent reading, and learning to read fluently, require a willingness to "make mistakes." And the extent to which a child is prepared to risk mistakes is directly related to the tolerance of the teacher in accepting them.

Many students who demonstrate an overreliance on text are the victims of intolerance (perhaps by teachers or parents who fail to see the benefit in helping students learn from their mistakes, or even by their own intolerance of uncertainty). This unwillingness to tolerate a normal amount of uncertainty obviously limits fluency and comprehension as well.

Calling for help or turning to reference sources every time a reader is uncertain of a piece of information is counterproductive. Readers need to give themselves a chance to interact with the author in a process of reducing uncertainty. What is an effective strategy for reducing uncertainty? Here's a four step approach that works for most purposes:

1. State the question or problem.
2. Form a tentative hypothesis. (Use the text as well as your world knowledge to make your best guess.)
3. Test your tentative hypothesis against subsequent information.
4. Accept your hypothesis as correct, or reject it and then consult appropriate reference resources (if important information is at stake).

Teachers should encourage students to take "educated" guesses when they experience uncertainty while reading. They should also provide constructive feedback to improve the quality of both questions and guesses.

Using context clues. Students at all levels can benefit from a knowledge of how writers provide definitions of key terms within the text of their writing. Author definitions within text can often provide enough information for learners so they do not always have to consult a dictionary. Showing readers how to acquire new vocabulary on their own is preferable to formal, teacher-directed vocabulary activities often conducted on the chalkboard. Readers should look for these (categories are from Thomas & Robinson, 1982, pp. 20-24) and other ways authors provide definitions of terms they consider to be important:

Direct explanation. Here the writer supplies an outright definition of a word the reader may not know. "A pond is usually stagnant—that is, the water is not mixed and churned" (Brandwein & others, 1975, p. 14).

Example. Near the unknown word an example throws light on the meaning. "In labor disputes, employers often shut down the factory until the workers accepted their terms. This was called a lockout" (Schwartz & O'Connor, 1971, p. 33).

Summary. Occasionally, the author may present the reader with an unfamiliar word which summarizes previously developed information and ideas. "These countries became known as 'satellites' of the Soviet Union." (Schwartz & O'Connor, 1971, p. 225).

Experience. From direct or vicarious experiences they may have had, readers know how people and things react in a given situation. "Her troubles were instantly at rest, her soul at peace again; for the indifference was broken up" (Twain, 1963, p. 141).

Language experience. Familiarity with common expressions can help the reader understand unfamiliar words. "The boy could not have shown a wilder, heartier interest if she had built a fire under him" (Twain, 1963, p. 141).

Mood. The meaning of the unfamiliar word should harmonize with the mood established in the rest of the passage. "The boy remained as dismal as a hearse" (Twain, 1963, p. 141).

Words in a series. Items or ideas enumerated in a series frequently share a common bond which may be recognized by the reader. "The conifers include trees such as firs, redwoods, yews, cypresses, junipers, cedars, pines, and spruces" (Brandwein & others, 1975, p. 250).

Synonyms. Here the unknown word repeats an idea expressed in words nearby. "The name conifer comes from two Latin words that mean cone bearer" (Brandwein & others, 1975, p. 250).

Comparison and/or contrast. The reader may discover the meaning of an unfamiliar word by comparing or contrasting it with familiar words nearby. "A living thing is not a jumble, like a pile of dust, or a rock" (Brandwein & others, 1975, p. 119).

Inference. The reader should be encouraged to reason out the meaning of a new word from the information and ideas at hand. With the exception of direct explanations, all authors' definitions require an educated guess on the part of the reader. "Just as every living cell must have oxygen, every living cell must give off its waste products. You know how the lungs expel carbon dioxide and water. Now consider the kidneys, the chief organs of the excretory system" (Brandwein & others, 1975, p. 118).

Failure to Make Text Based Inferences

Students who fail to find information which seems to be staring them in the face may lack sufficient knowledge about language to "read between the lines." The specific linguistic structures used to express a given idea may vary greatly from writer to writer. Teachers should review the readings they assign to determine the kinds of demands the writing style and vocabulary may place upon students' language processing skills. Failure to make inferences based upon information directly stated in the text is one signal that learners may be unfamiliar with the writer's use of language.

English teachers, foreign language specialists, and elementary school language arts teachers are probably already familiar with how the writer's language can influence the "readability" of written discourse. Basic linguistic structures are outlined in this section as a brief introduction for those teachers who may have a limited background in what to look for as they review print material. Direct teaching of this material is unnecessary for most students; reserve explanations for those students who experience comprehension failure due to unfamiliar writing styles.

Basic Linguistic Structures

I. Forms of Sentences
A complete thought may be expressed in different ways:
  A. *Active*—Walter invited Michelle to the reception.
  B. *Passive*—Michelle was invited to the reception by Walter.
  C. *Interrogative*—Wasn't Michelle invited to the reception by Walter?

Some students experience more difficulty with the passive and interrogative sentence forms than they do with the active form.

II. Transformational Processes
  A. *Adjunction*—contracting and adjoining one word to another within a sentence:
  Michelle *will not* attend the reception with Walter.
  Michelle *won't* attend the reception with Walter.
  B. *Substitution*—the exchange of one noun or noun phrase for another of functional equivalence:
  Michelle is fun to be with.
  It is fun to be with Michelle.
  C. *Deletion*—nouns and verbs may be left out of the text without altering the writer's message by deletion:
  I will come to your party, and Michelle will come to your party.
  I will come to your party, and Michelle will too.

III. Verbs and Connectives
  A. *Verbs*—the verb is the focal point for a large portion of the message within a sentence:
  The kick hurt Tom.
  Lois hurt Doug.
  Wars hurt the nation.
  B. *Connectives*—serve meaningful as well as structural functions within sentences. Besides marking the direction of the writer's ideas, connectives help the reader anticipate the content of subsequent text:
  Michelle would like to come over, but she can't.
  Michelle wants to come over, so she will.

IV. Clauses

Clauses are grammatical structures which often refer to theme, transitivity (situations in which the verb requires a compliment to complete its meaning), and/or modality (the mood of the situation). The reader must frequently hold a subordinate idea in mind prior to reading the major point in the sentence—the coordinate idea:

"But there are such things as intentional mistakes or oversights, and, as it happens, Jules Verne, who also knew a thing or two in assorted sciences—and had, besides, a surprising amount of prophetic power—deliberately seems to make the same mistake that Professor Goddard seems to make" (Clymer & others, 1970, p. 203).

V. Anaphora

Anaphora employs pronouns, auxiliary verbs, etc., in a sort of grammatical cross-reference system running the gamut from substituting the referent *she* for a woman's name mentioned previously, to such a predicate referent as *they do too.*

"Computerized diagnosis has resulted in another major medical breakthrough—'telemedicine'. Telemedicine is the examination of patients by way of long distance telephone. This new use of computers requires fewer doctors. It has helped many patients living outside major cities to 'see' specialists over great distances" (Early & others, 1979, p. 206).

This and *it* refer to the several examples of diagnostic devices mentioned earlier in the selection, as well as to the term "telemedicine." *See* refers to the process of receiving a physician's care (from an eighth grade skills reader).

Closure Techniques

All people learn by trial and error. When presented with a problem, we try the most plausible solutions which present themselves, observe the effects of our actions, and repeat the process until we have achieved a satisfactory approximation of an "answer." This process of reducing uncertainty is commonly referred to as "the learning process." One flexible and powerful approach to developing the learning process is the use of closure. This procedure is an application of the principle emphasized by gestalt psychologists as "the perceptions of incomplete figures or situations as though complete by ignoring the missing parts or by compensating for them by projection based on past experience"

(Webster's Third New International Dictionary of the English Language: Unabridged, 1976, p. 438).

Elegant in their simplicity, closure techniques can be used by teachers to structure a great variety of learning "problems" for their students to solve. The teacher creates a closure exercise by deleting selected portions of the text, leaving empty spaces which the learner must fill. The reader's "best guess" represents the product of a complex process of approximation. A few of the previously cited context clue examples will be converted to show how typical closure exercises are constructed.

To help the student understand anaphoric relationships, delete the referent: This is the ride for _____ (me we she). Notice that the reader must choose among three alternatives. Two choices may just as well have been provided, as in this choice between two connectives: Everything went well _____ the Liberty Bell 7 landed at sea fifteen minutes after launching (until but). Ordinarily, the lines are drawn of uniform length; word length alone does not govern the choice. The multiple choice activity can be used for anaphora and connectives as above, for subordinate clauses, verbs, and author's definitions—for any identifiable unit of written language for that matter.

When the closure exercise is constructed without given choices, more of the burden of reducing uncertainty falls upon the student. This kind of closure exercise is more of a challenge to the learner: The boy could not have shown a wilder, _____ interest if she had built a fire under him. The boy remained as _____ as a hearse.

Notice that each of the sentences above requires an adjective for completion. This reduces uncertainty with respect to syntactic considerations. Language experience and mood clues reduce uncertainty with respect to semantic considerations. Should the reader's "best guess" prove insufficient, the teacher should provide assistance as necessary to ensure understanding. Rather than simply giving the answer, the teacher should try to provide only the minimum information the learner needs in order to approximate an acceptable solution. The kind of information needed should help guide the teacher in the construction of subsequent exercises.

Peers are often very helpful to each other in reviewing each other's responses in closure tasks. Discussions of which answer seems most pertinent, closest to the author's words, or most logical help to develop language awareness. Closure tasks play an important role in helping students make text based inferences.

Overreliance on One Set of Strategies

Effective readers monitor and regulate their progress throughout the completion of study assignments. Keeping in mind the purpose(s) established prior to reading while processing the writer's presentation helps students match their most efficient strategies to the varying demands of each specific task. We have discussed a number of study skills and strategies which should be part of every student's portfolio. Some students fail to make use of their most efficient strategies. These students habitually rely upon one set of strategies to complete a wide variety of assignments. They may succeed in completing their assignments, but students who use only one set of strategies must be willing to spend extra time and effort to do the job.

Higher Education Demands Flexibility

James was an honors student in high school, and looked forward to a full and rewarding freshman year as an Ivy League university student. He was understandably disappointed to find that the academic demands of his course work made him a virtual hermit on campus. Even more disappointing was the fact that despite his great investment in study time, James' grades were not outstanding. James' read-reread study strategy had always worked in high school, but now there was just too great a volume of difficult assignments for his one set of strategies to be effective. James found out the hard way how an overreliance on one set of strategies can undermine efficiency.

How does inefficiency result in failure? Students who fail to monitor or regulate their use of study strategies often experience failure when a number of demanding assignments must be completed within a limited time. This kind of problem may first surface when students who had been very successful in using one set of strategies to complete one teacher's assignments in elementary school suddenly begin to have problems finishing the work assigned by several subject teachers in junior or senior high. As the volume of work increases, these otherwise serious students may display a tendency to resist or complain about assignments which they consider demand "too much work" or "too much time" to complete. These students may actually be trying to tell us that they don't know how to get their work done efficiently. Some teachers compound this problem by holding students responsible for trivial details unrelated to the expressed purpose(s) of the assignment.

The end result can be that these students may resist making their contribution to the comprehension process. Here are a couple of things you can do to help these students:

    A. Make students aware of the need to monitor and regulate their study strategies according to their purpose(s) and the nature of the material. Stress *flexibility*.

Students who have a clear purpose for reading know what they're looking for. Those who have been shown how to locate key information and ideas can expect to find what they're looking for. Taken together, these factors contribute a good deal to the rate at which a student will read. The more efficiently readers find what they're looking for, the less time the entire process takes. But this does *not* mean reading at the same rate all the time. Readers should have not one, but several rates of reading. Developing flexibility of rate—speeding up and slowing down as necessary—is the goal to impress upon your students. Here is some advice adapted from Thomas and Robinson (1979, pp. 10-11, 15) which will be useful for students.

Can You Adjust Your Reading Rate to the Task at Hand?

1. Shift from one rate and method to another in view of these considerations:
   a. Your purpose
      Why are you reading this material?
      - To get just the gist of an easy selection?
      - To learn, point by point, a specific process or a detailed sequence?
      - To find one particular point in a selection you've already read?
      - To entertain yourself with light, easy reading?
   b. What is the difficulty of the material for you?
      - Is it easy?
      - Is it rough going?
   c. How familiar are you with the subject matter?
      - Do you already have background on the topic?
      - Is it new to you?

2. You should have in your collection of rates the following approaches:

Approach	How Fast	When to Use
Scanning, not a true reading rate—just glancing until you find what you want	*Maybe* 1500 or more words words per minute (rate is an individual matter)	When glancing down pages to find a single piece of information
Skimming (previewing or overviewing), not a true reading rate—just getting the gist of the article, hitting the high points.	*Maybe* 800-1000 words per minute	To get the general content of an article, "What it's all about?"
Actual Reading Rates		
a. Very rapid	*Maybe* 500 words per minute	For light, easy fast-moving fiction reading
b. Rapid	*Maybe* 350 words per minute	For fairly easy materials when you want only the more important facts, ideas
c. Average	*Perhaps* 250 words per minute	For magazine articles such as *Science Digest*; some chapters in social studies; some travel books; some novels like *My Antonia* or *Cry the Beloved Country*
d. Slow and Careful	From 250 words per minute, all the way down to a *slow* 50 words per minute or *even slower*	For difficult concepts and vocabulary, for thorough reading of technical matter, for retaining every detail, for weighing the truth of difficult reading. (Here "thought time" is needed in addition to reading time.)

3. You may need to shift from one rate (and approach) to another *within a single chapter* of a textbook or within an article—even within a single paragraph. This shifting of speed within a selection is called *internal rate adjustment*. Let's suppose, for example, you're reading a chapter in science, "Fish and Fishlike Vertebrates." The introduction is a narrative—the story of how deadly eel-like sea lampreys invaded the Great Lakes. Read this fairly fast. The body of the chapter is closely packed with information. Reduce speed. Later you find some easy paragraphs on sport fishing as a hobby. Speed up again.

   Certain passages say, "speed up your reading" while others say, "slow down." You'll want to shift from one speed to another *within a passage*—even within a single paragraph. These signals should help you adjust your speed appropriately.

Graham and Robinson

a. *Speed-up signals*
   1. An easy passage—no vocabulary blocks, no complicated sentences or concepts.
   2. A passage from which you want to obtain only the most important ideas.
   3. A passage that merely repeats or elaborates something you've already grasped, or an example or illustration that drives home a point you already understand.
   4. A light, easy passage within a longer selection, one that changes the pace of more difficult material.
   5. Subject matter on which you're already well-informed.
   6. Subject matter unrelated to your present purpose.
b. *Slow-down signals*
   1. Difficult new terms or concepts that block your understanding.
   2. Difficult technical material you want to master.
   3. Details you want to retain.
   4. Subject matter that is new territory for you—when you lack background information.
   5. Directions you are to follow precisely.
   6. Material that contains a diagram or other pictorial aid, requiring shifting of eyes and thoughts from the printed words to the graphic aid.
   7. Material that requires visualizing time—when you must form an "eye picture" of what you are reading.
   8. Ideas you want to weigh thoroughly—when "thought time" is needed in addition to reading time.
   9. Artistic writing that invites you to linger.
   10. Words you want to "live by."

B. Vary the kinds of work you assign, and show students how to complete their assignments efficiently. Simulate *how* an efficient reader would approach each task.
   • The teacher can play the role of a student about to complete the home study task just assigned, acting out and explaining each step in the process. Inefficient strategies may be discussed for comparison, and to illustate specific difficulties which may be anticipated or experienced during the completion of the assignment.
   • Students may put themselves in the place of their teacher or classmates by making constructive criticism of the

activities they observe. A form can be prepared and distributed to solicit the kinds of feedback desired.

Name _____   Activity _____
Date _____   Presenter _____

Constructive Criticism Sheet

Directions: Answer each of the following questions as you take part in this class activity. Include any information which you feel would help improve the activity.
1. What was the purpose of this activity?
2. Was the purpose accomplished?
3. Were there any problems with the presentation?
4. How might these problems have been avoided or overcome?
5. How could this activity be improved?

- Students can prepare activities for peer tutoring of classmates or younger students. The teacher can supervise these activities and help students learn about their own strategies while they are helping others.

Reaction Guide

The three views of the reading process presented earlier in this chapter differ mainly in terms of the reader's contribution to the process of gaining new information and ideas from print. Most theoretical models of the reading process (including yours and your students') are characterized by where they place the reader along a continuum ranging from very passive to very active.

Directions. Illustrate the kind of imbalance which each problem discussed in this chapter indicates by "tilting" the scale in the direction of the imbalance. Then indicate ways teachers may help restore the balance according to suggestions made in this chapter. The first one is done for you.

1) *Overreliance on Prior Knowledge*
   Too ————————— Too
   a. Passive   Δ ——————Active
   b. Way(s) to restore balance:
      differentiate assignments

2) *Overreliance on Text*
       Too   Too
   a. Passive   Δ   Active
   b. Way(s) to restore balance:

   _____

   _____

3) *Failure to Make Text Based Inferences*
       Too   Too
   a. Passive   Δ   Active
   b. Way(s) to restore balance:

   _____

   _____

4) *Overreliance on One Set of Strategies*
       Too   Too
   a. Passive   Δ   Active
   b. Way(s) to restore balance:

   _____

   _____

Answers to Pre- and Postorganizers

Study Guide

I.		II.		III.	
√	a.	√	a.	___	a.
√	b.	√	b.	√	b.
___	c.	___	c.	√	c.
√	d.	√	d.	√	d.
___	e.	___	e.	___	e.

Reaction Guide

    Too   Too
2) a. Passive   Δ   Active
    b. Answers will vary

    Too   Too
3) a. Passive   Δ   Active
    b. Answers will vary

    Too   Too
4) a. Passive   Δ   Active
    b. Answers will vary

Chapter 4
AFTER THE EYES LEAVE THE PAGE

Divided Page

Directions: Read each of the following questions, then skim the chapter to find the page(s) on which the answer(s) may be found. Write the correct page number(s) in the space(s) provided. Then read each section and write the answer to each question in the appropriate answer space. The first one is done for you.

Page Nos.	Questions	Answers
p. 97 / 100	What important purpose(s) can class discussions serve?	• Linking pre- and postorganizers • Helping students learn from each other
p. _____ / _____	How might students' retention strategies be improved?	_____
p. _____ / _____	What five test taking strategies should teachers recommend to their students?	1. _____ 2. _____ 3. _____ 4. _____ 5. _____
p. _____ / _____	What are four main steps in the report writing process?	1. _____ 2. _____ 3. _____ 4. _____
p. _____ / _____	What does PQ5R stand for?	P. _____ Q. _____ R. _____ R. _____ R. _____ R. _____ R. _____
p. _____	What is the purpose of the divided page technique?	_____

Correct answers appear at end of chapter.

Questions and Answers

Q. Why do some students always seem to gain more from completing study assignments than others in the same class?

A. Learners differ in their general and specific preparedness for study tasks (as discussed in Chapters 1 and 2), and in their development and application of effective language processing strategies for completing specific study assignments (as discussed in Chapter 3). Learners also differ in how well they express the information and ideas they have gained as a result of their study. Some students are better at "showing what they know" than others. Students who are less able at expressing themselves are at a disadvantage. Teachers can help students improve their students' communication skills as part of every lesson they teach. In this chapter we explain how.

Q. I am frequently disappointed with the poor test scores of some of my better readers. I'm sure they have a good understanding of their readings, and their parents assure me that they study at home. Why don't they earn the grades they should?

A. Preparing for and taking a test requires skills (such as following directions, budgeting time, etc.) which are separate and apart from those needed to gain new information and ideas from print. Students who have not learned how to prepare for and take a test may not truly deserve the poor grades they may earn. Students' grades should be reflections of what they have learned. In some cases, test grades may only reflect what students don't know about preparing for and taking tests.

Q. My students seem to do a "rush job" when reports are assigned. I have shown them how to organize their study time, so why don't they get their work done before the last minute?

A. Unfortunately, many students do avoid writing reports until the last minute. Some underestimate the amount of time they actually need to complete a report properly. Others lose so much time to ineffective and inefficient report writing strategies that they are unable or unwilling to complete their reports on time. Teachers at all grade levels (from first grade show and tell to senior term papers) can help students develop the skills they need to complete report writing assignments on their own.

Before and After

Preorganizing activities (before the eyes hit the page) and postorganizing activities (after the eyes have left the page) must be connected. When reading material is being used as an instrument of instruction, students should not be surprised by a multitude of unexpected questions or activities after reading. Students will learn best if what they were guided to anticipate becomes expectation.

We have tried, in this volume, to provide several different types of preorganizers and postorganizers for your use. We have also mentioned a number of preorganizers (anticipatory questions, semantic organizers, study guides) that can also become postorganizers. For example, the following semantic organizer (a sequence organizer) was developed by a group *before* they read a story about the life cycle of frogs.

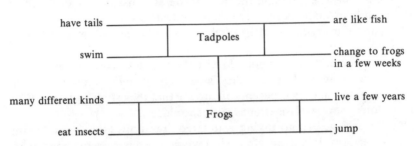

The group felt they didn't know very much about the life cycle of the frog but went to the story looking to confirm what they did know and to find additional information.

After the reading of the story, each student was asked to correct, refine, and expand the preorganizer. Here is one student's revision.

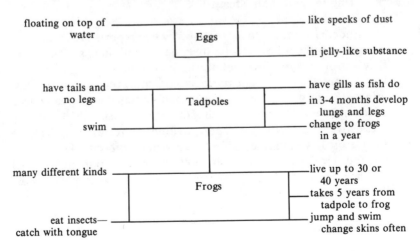

Graham and Robinson

After each student revised the preorganizer, the group decided to collaborate on one postorganizer. They did, indeed, learn about the life cycle of the frog.

In the remainder of this chapter we have concentrated our attention on class discussions, retention tasks, test taking strategies, and report writing as postorganizing activities students must learn to cope with. Such activities are important challenges for most learners.

Class Discussion

Developing independent learners involves building confidence— and to many students, confidence means being letter clear about the demands to be made of them before they begin reading. Having to wait until after they have finished reading to receive the teacher's questions encourages teacher-dependence—students passively waiting for the teacher's questions rather than actively seeking the writer's answers. Students who have learned to equate success with satisfying initial purposes for reading have developed a powerful independent study strategy. Unrelated or trick questions posed after reading add nothing to the information-gathering process, and actually may serve to undermine confidence by discouraging independence. What takes place after the eyes leave the page can exert a powerful influence upon how students view the entire study process.

Comprehension is the result of an interaction between reader and writer which often consists of ideas and information retained, organized, and expressed after the eyes have left the page of print. Because many reading comprehension activities are conducted with the book closed, demonstrating comprehension after reading demands a set of strategies which are separate and apart from those involved in unlocking meaning while the eyes are on the page. Students need to be shown how to deal effectively with discussions, tests, and written assignments based on material previously read.

Questions and discussions directly related to prereading purposes might be called anticipatory comprehension. We suggested earlier that teachers and students engage in specific readiness activities in order to help bridge the gap between the background of the reader and the new information and ideas presented by the writer. Preorganizers help insure that the meaning search will have been active and purposeful. Anticipatory comprehension relates to the kind of information and ideas students are expected to have acquired as a direct result of having satisfied initial purposes for reading. The concept of anticipatory comprehension is rooted in the idea that students should be able to anticipate the kinds of questions their teacher will ask at the completion of a given study assignment.

However, class discussion can accomplish more than simply the review of preorganizers. Ancient scholars feared that active dialogue would become a lost art if reading and writing became popular. Active, personal involvement and interaction were considered to be essential components of the learning process. We can take a cue from our ancestors by helping students learn from each other through class discussion.

Tips for Guiding Class Discussion

1. Guide the students' discussion—don't lead it yourself.
2. Take care to see that each student gets an opportunity to participate.
3. Allow students time to prepare for the discussion of specific topics or certain questions—not broad, general areas of common knowledge.
4. Differentiate assignments—vary the difficulty of the assignment to suit the ability of the individual student.
5. Direct the students back into the text as necessary for reference.
6. Encourage students to use media aids, such as the chalkboard, in their presentations.
7. Establish some form of "discussion etiquette" or parliamentary procedure.
8. Allow time after the discussion for self-evaluation and constructive criticism of peers.
9. Take time to review the important points of the discussion and how they were made.
10. Monitor the ways in which students organize and present information and ideas: Are the purposes clear? Is material presented logically? Are major points highlighted?

Retention

Students often need help in learning to retain what they comprehend. Some students understand material only when they have it before them, but have not developed effective strategies for committing key information and ideas to memory for use when the book is closed. The traditional ways in which comprehension is

Graham and Robinson

measured place a large demand upon memory of material previously read. For this reason, students with poor retention strategies often earn poor grades on comprehension tasks. But students often understand more than they retain. While their eyes are on the page, students can make use of the writer's scheme of organization. After their eyes leave the page, students must organize information and ideas they wish to retain according to a scheme of their own.

How might retention be improved? Retention means organizing and storing information in a way that makes for adequate recall. Students find it difficult to keep in mind what they don't understand in the first place. Teachers can show students how to organize and store information by showing them how to make use of the techniques of categorization, personalization, application, and self-recitation. These techniques may be used alone or in combination to improve retention of material previously read:

Categorization—associating the new information within a context of which it is a part, such as connecting the kinkajou to other marsupials in the student's experience (like the kangaroo).

Personalization—associating the new information within the context of the student's personal experiences, such as associating a vocabulary word (precocious) with a person known to the student.

Application—making use of or building experience around material learned, such as making a model or diarama.

Self-Recitation—making use of all sensory channels through repetition, mnemonics, etc.

Test Taking

Traditional forms of comprehension measurement include tests and written work, although games and simulations, dramatics, and other nonprint forms may also be used to measure comprehension. Each form of comprehension measurement is meant to determine how well material read was understood and retained. Students differ in how well they understand what they are reading while their eyes are on the page. They also differ in how well they can retain, organize, and express what they understand after their eyes leave the page of print. As a result, students must be shown how to approach different kinds of comprehension tasks.

Students at all grade levels are called upon to take tests and give reports based upon material learned in the course of completing study assignments. We have taken note of individual differences among students with respect to general and specific readiness considerations. In light of these factors we have suggested strategies for improving communication between reader and writer—before and while their eyes are on the page of print. In taking a test, the teacher must weigh these factors and their interrelationships in light of content and process goals and objectives. Taking a test should be a learning experience in itself. Teachers should show students how to deal effectively with this most demanding activity.

Many factors which are not directly related to the information-gathering process come into play when tests are to be taken. Expressing information and ideas retained in memory during a test demands higher-level skills than those necessary for locating key information and ideas while reading. Teachers should not casually assume that if students understand what they read they will automatically do well on any test. Left to their own devices, students often develop inefficient and ineffective strategies in response to the pressure of competing for grades. Showing students how to take tests helps reduce the kind of stress commonly observed when tests are administered. This set of "how to take a test" ideas covers the basics students need to know about showing what they've learned.

Test Taking Strategies

Do the words, "Unit test next Friday" or "Final exam in three weeks" still make you uneasy? Does the familiar instruction, "Clear your desks," always seem to signal a test? Do you remember reading the first question on a test and then getting a sudden attack of "temporary amnesia"? If any of these situations sound vaguely familiar, then you will want to pay careful attention to the strategies which follow.

I. *Find out about the test beforehand, and prepare for it in advance.* Find the answers to these questions as soon as possible after the test has been announced.
   A. *What topics will be included?*
      1. Study each topic separately, and budget your study time to review each topic twice before the test.
      2. Short study sessions spread over a period of time usually work better than marathon study sessions just before the test. Study groups, with a few serious friends, work well for some students.

B. *Which specific notes and readings will be included?*
1. Review your notes first, then refer to the readings to clear up any confusion. Here's where taking good notes pays off.
2. Use the buddy system to quiz yourself on the specific information and ideas in your notes. Classmates, friends, or family members can help you study by asking and answering questions from your notes and readings.
C. *How many and what kinds of questions will be asked?*
1. Expect to work quickly when many questions are to be asked. Don't wait until the paper is on your desk to find out the size of the test. Students have been known to "freeze" in the face of large tests they didn't expect.
2. Knowing the kind(s) of questions to be asked can help relieve some of the stress and strain tests have been known to produce:
   a. *Multiple choice, matching,* and *true/false* questions provide you with the answers; your job is to select the correct one.
   b. *Modified true/false* and *fill-in* questions don't provide the answers; that's up to you. Usually the correct answer is a certain fact or detail.
   c. *Essay* questions usually call for memory of major topics and supporting details, personal reactions, and good organizational and writing skills. Knowing the answer is not enough—how you present what you know is also important.
D. *How much time will be allowed to complete the test?*
1. Some students work faster than others. Plan to finish the test even if you are ordinarily a slow worker. Spending extra time studying at home can make things go faster during the test. Answer the questions you are sure of first, then go back and finish the rest. The more you study, the more questions you are likely to get right the first time around.
2. Plan to check your work if you finish early.
E. *How much will this test count toward the final grade?*
1. Ordinarily, the more a test counts toward the final grade, the more difficult it will be (more topics, more questions, and more difficult questions). Therefore, it makes sense to give the "big test" more study time.
2. "Little" tests add up, so make time to study for them too.

F. *Are any special supplies needed?*
   1. Be prepared! If the test calls for a pen, and you show up with a pencil it can cost points. If the test is open book or open notebook, and yours is at home, it can cost points. You have a responsibility to find out what is required and then to meet those requirements.
II. *Give the test a "once-over" before you begin.*
   A. Make sure you have all pages, answer sheets, scrap paper, etc.
   B. Determine how many and what kind of questions are to be answered.
   C. Determine how much "weight" each question carries.
   D. Rank each part of the test in terms of difficulty for *you.*
III. *Budget your time.*
   A. Estimate how long each part will take you to finish.
   B. Compare your estimate with the time allowed.
   C. Plan to do the easiest parts for you first—save the hardest parts for last.
   D. Check the time after each part is completed.
   E. Leave yourself time to review your work.
IV. *Read directions and follow them carefully. Learn the language of test directions.*
   A. Some directions apply to the whole test.
      1. *Directions:* All parts. Do all work on the answer sheet provided. Answer essay questions on separate composition paper.
      2. Write the letter of the answer that best completes the sentence or answers the question on the answer sheet. Do not write answers on this paper.
      3. All the answers are to be put on the answer sheet. You can write on the question pages, but final work must be on the answer sheet only.
   B. Some directions apply only to certain parts of the test.
      1. Part One—multiple choice: This part of the examination will test your ability to recall scientific facts, concepts, and principles. Select the term that best completes each of the following statements. Then place the letter that is in front of the term on the answer sheet. Answer all questions (80) in this part.   (40 points)
      2. Part Three—This part consists of eight "groups." Each group contains 5 questions. Choose only 5 out of these 8 groups. Write all answers on the separate answer sheet. Base

all answers on the information or diagram that is supplied with the "group." (25 points)

3. Directions: All three of the following essays must be completed. Essays are to be written on white composition paper, using proper essay form and correct English grammar. Be certain that all parts of each essay are complete.

C. Other directions serve to explain specific kinds of questions.

1. Multiple Choice
Directions: In the proper space on your answer sheet, place the letter of the choice which best completes the statement or answers the question.

2. Matching
Directions: In the space provided on the answer sheet, place the letter of the description from column B which best fits the person named in column A.

3. True/False
Directions: Read the following statements. Write the word true in the blank space beside each statement that is true. Write the word false in the blank space beside each statement that is false.

4. Modified True/False
Directions: On your answer sheet write true if the statement is true. If the statement is false, change the underlined word to make it true.

5. Fill-In (or Short Answer)
Directions: Complete each statement below with the word or words which will make it true. Write each answer in the blank space provided on the answer sheet.

6. Essay
Directions: You must select one topic from Part A, and you must select one topic from Part B. Be sure to organize each essay with a topic paragraph, a body, and a conclusion.

V. *Vary your approach to suit different kinds of questions.*

A. Answer all questions you are sure of first. Save the hardest questions for last so that you don't run out of time with "easy" questions unanswered.

B. Use the process of elimination to improve your chances of guessing difficult multiple choice and matching questions. Example: White light can be broken up into the colors of the spectrum by a (a) lens (b) mirror (c) prism (d) hammer and chisel. Most students know that *b* and *d* can be eliminated, improving the chance of making a correct guess. Matching questions are best dealt with in a similar way.

C. Be sure to read all choices before writing your answer. Example: Friction is an advantage in which of the following? (a) bicycle brakes (b) walking (c) holding a pen (d) all of the above. While each individual answer is correct, choice *d* is the best answer. Do not write an answer until you have read all choices.

D. Take special care to note key words which set conditions. Example: In order for a sound wave to be produced, all of the following are necessary except a) a force must be applied, b) an absence of matter, c) an object must vibrate, d) molecules must be present. The key words here are *all* and *except*, which set the conditions under which the statement is true. When answering True/False and Modified True/False questions, bear in mind that true statements must always be true. For example, Fear is always bad. (True or False) The key word here is *always*, making the statement false.

E. Search the test for clues to fill-in or short answer questions you are not sure of. A question such as
- A disease associated with heavy drinking is _____ .
may be answered in another part of the test.
- Alcoholism is a disease which can be treated. Patients must refrain from drinking as part of their therapy. Explain the effects of alcoholism upon the central nervous system.

F. Make a rough draft of essays, and proofread to be sure you have answered the question. Some students get so involved in writing an essay that they neglect to answer the question. Answer the question first, then rewrite your rough draft in good essay form.
Example: Many books have been made into successful movies or TV shows. In a well organized essay, tell why *David Copperfield* could be successfully made into a movie or TV show. Include at least three scenes that would be interesting to watch. Be sure to give reasons for your choices.

Notice that essay questions involve more than just remembering facts and specific details. You must draw upon your personal knowledge and experiences as well as your understanding of what you have read in order to give a complete answer.

Graham and Robinson

Report Writing

Many students find report writing to be a difficult and time consuming chore. Some feel they are wasting their time in writing a report, and suspect that they probably couldn't do a good job if they wanted to. As a result, many reports get put off until shortly before they are due. The last-minute shortcuts taken by some students range from throwing themselves upon the mercy of a friendly and helpful librarian to "borrowing" the talents of others for an assignment they should complete alone.

Not every student avoids writing reports—some find report writing interesting, challenging, and rewarding (as well they should)! Those who resist usually fall into one of two groups: those who *can't* write a good report, and those who *won't* write a good report. Our job is to make the report writing jobs we assign interesting, challenging, and rewarding for all our students. It may take a little doing, but it can be done (which can help make teaching the interesting, challenging, and rewarding experience it should be, too)! All students need to learn how to handle report writing assignments. Of course, it would be a tall order to expect students to learn everything they need to know at one time.

Sometimes a little soul-searching on the part of the teacher before the report is assigned can help streamline the entire process for all concerned. Ask yourself:

- What is my purpose in assigning this report?
- Which content and process goals and objectives will be achieved?
- How ready are my students for this task?
- Will what the students learn from this experience be worth the time and energy it will take?

If you are not absolutely sure of the answers to these questions, then you may be assured that your students will have their doubts as well.

Students are assigned relatively few reports in the course of a term, yet each report may carry the weight of a large test in determining a final grade. Students vary considerably in how they respond to the pressures (such as due dates and grades) associated with written assignments. Several of the test-taking strategies previously described can be readily applied to the report writing situation (budgeting time, for example). But the major concern of the teacher should be in showing students how to locate, select, organize, and express key information and ideas on their own. Simply requiring that students submit a certain number of pages on a given topic doesn't help get the job done. Teaching report writing strategies can.

Report Writing Strategies

One kind of assignment that every student faces at one time or another is writing a report. Do you find report writing interesting, challenging, and rewarding? If your answer is "Yes" then you have probably developed a system for writing reports that works for you. Unfortunately, many students would answer "No!" to the above question. Why? Well, usually for one of two reasons: 1) they haven't developed a system of writing a report that works for them or 2) they don't understand the purpose or importance of the assignment (it may not be meaningful for them). If you find report writing worthwhile, the information which follows may teach you a few new tricks. If you are one of the students who avoids writing reports, the information which follows should be of great interest to you. Why? Because it will describe a system for writing reports that can work for *you.* Once you know *how* to write a report, it becomes easier to understand the importance of a particular assignment.

Be sure you get all the information you can about the nature of the assignment before you begin. Having clear purpose(s) in mind at the start will make the job easier to finish.

Questions to Ask before Writing a Report

1. What topic(s) should be included?
2. How many and what kind of reference sources should be used?
3. How much time will be allowed to complete this report?
4. How much will this report count toward the final grade?
5. What are the minimum and maximum lengths the finished report should be?
6. Is there a particular form or style in which the report should be written?
7. Are graphic aids required?
8. What purpose or specific goal should writing this report accomplish?
9. Is there an example of an excellent report available which may be used as a model?
10. Am I ready to complete this assignment? If the answer is "yes," then get started! If the answer is "no," then read on.

Writing a report is a four step process: Step 1—LOCATE your sources. Step 2—SELECT key information and ideas. Step 3—ORGANIZE according to your purpose(s). Step 4—EXPRESS your meaning as best you can. Let's take a look at this process step by step.

Graham and Robinson

Step 1. Locate Your Sources

Sources of written information may be separated into two groups: those we call primary sources and those we call secondary sources.

Primary sources are novels, short stories, poetry, drama, and nonfiction written by original authors (a novel by Judy Blume, or a research article by Einstein are examples of primary sources). The word primary means first—you get the information firsthand!

Secondary sources are interpretations of the original author's work by a writer other than the original author (a review of Judy Blume's new novel, or an encyclopedia entry explaining Einstein's work, for example). You can save time in the library if you know what kind of sources you are looking for when you arrive.

The library stores a great deal of information from many sources, and keeps this information organized by author, title, and subject in the card catalog. If you want to see a listing of all of Judy Blume's books, just look under "B" in the *author* index of the card catalog (B for Blume, the author's last name). If you know of a certain book you want to find, just look for it by name in the *title* index of the card catalog. If your assignment calls for primary sources, then the author and title index should help you locate the information you need. But very often you are assigned a report topic, rather than a specific author or book to report on. How are you supposed to know which of the books in the library has information on the topic of your report? Wouldn't it be nice if someone read every book and then wrote down what it was about and the topics it discussed? Actually, the *subject* index in the card catalog does just that. Just look for the name of your topic (usually a word or phrase) in the subject index of the card catalog and you should find the names of books with information on your topic.

Once you find the book you're looking for in the card catalog, your next job is to find out where your book is located in the library bookcases. The library numbers each book so that you can find it easily. The bookcases are labeled with the numbers of the books they hold. This numbering system is called the Dewey Decimal System. Books on the same subject are given the same number (which makes it easier for report writers like you to locate your sources of information). Only fiction books (like novels by Judy Blume) have no numbers; they are organized in the bookcases alphabetically, by the author's last name.

Suppose you don't find your topic listed in the subject index of the card catalog? It is very likely that your report topic goes by a different name in the subject index. It is helpful to make a list of the different names your topic may be known by (car and automobile, for example). When you can't think of any other names for your topic, check the dictionary, encyclopedia, or thesaurus. These books may not have much information on your topic, but the information they do give can help you make a list of related terms to describe your topic. Now go back and re-search the card catalog—you'll probably find more books than you need.

Other points of interest for the library researcher:

- Librarians and teachers are trained resource people, which means they know how to help you find the material you need for your report (remember, help you find does not mean find for you...).
- Leave yourself plenty of time to find your way around the library until you get used to it. Beginners take longer.
- Don't sign out every book you find; be selective. (More on this in the next step.)
- If you can't find a book you need, check at the circulation desk (someone else may be using it).
- Don't give up; take a break instead.

Step 2. Select Key Information and Ideas

Before you actually sit down and read the material you collect during your library research, you should try to select the best sources of information. But how are you supposed to know which sources of information are best? You can't judge a book by its cover, the old saying goes. But how do you judge a book when you have a report to write? Don't settle for the first book you find but don't try to read every book you find, either. Try this "brainstorming" technique first:

1. Write down your report topic _____
   (word or phrase only)
2. Add a few words to make your purpose in writing the report clear _____
   The best way to say what you intend to do is to use action words such as compare, contrast, evaluate, explain, analyze, interpret, define, describe, identify, discuss, summarize. You might also talk your ideas over with a friend, relative, teacher, or librarian in order to arrive at a clear statement of your purposes in writing the report.
3. Use your experience (what you already know about the topic) to describe what you expect your finished report will be about, in sentence form this time _____

Be sure your sentence tells who, what, where, when, why, and how. If you don't have enough experience with your topic to say what you expect your report to be about, then you're not ready to select the best sources of information. You can gain some experience by reading brief articles that have to do with your topic in reference books. Experience also can be gained from other sources, such as films and television. Find out enough about your topic to say what interests you about it. Don't write the title yet though, you don't always find what you expect. Now that you know what you're looking for, choose your best sources.

Scan the index of each book for general topics you used when searching the subject index of the card catalog. Read each entry to find the pages which deal with your specific topic. Check cross-references if they seem promising. Now turn to the pages which deal with your specific topic and skim to get a general idea of their content.

Jot down the name of each book that seems to have information you can use on an index card. Make a note of specific page numbers and any special features that interest you (a map or diagram, for example). When you have done this for all the books you were able to locate, you should be able to select the best sources to actually read for your report. Sign these books out of the library. Make a readings list for yourself, and budget enough time to read and take notes on the selected pages of the best sources you have found.

Take notes as you complete each reading. Jot down key information and ideas on index cards. If you want to use the author's exact words in your report, jot them down within quotes (" ") and make a note of the page number on which you found them. Using the author's words in your report is called making a direct quote. If you decide to change the author's words, but keep the author's meaning, make a note of the page number. Using your words for the author's meaning is called making an indirect quote, or paraphrase. You may prefer to write an original paragraph or two after each reading. This is called a summary.

When you have completed all your readings, review your notes. Use a yellow felt pen or other marker to highlight the most important information you have found. If you find that some of your notes are duplicates, select the best and eliminate the rest. If you really haven't found enough information to accomplish your purposes, go back to the library and search again. You should have enough experience by now to know what you're looking for and how to find it.

Step 3. Organize According to Your Purposes

Now that you're an "expert" on your topic, it is time to plan the best way to communicate what you know to others. First, decide which broad pattern(s) of writing best fits the kind of information and ideas you want to get across (you can choose more than one). The pattern you choose should help you do what the action words in your specific topic say you will do.

Comparison and/or contrast. Do you intend to show how two or more things are alike and/or different? First, list each item to be compared and its important characteristics. Next, list the similarities among the items on your list. Finally, list the differences between them. Save your list for reference.

General statement/details. Do you intend to make a statement that you believe to be true in most cases? Should others be persuaded to agree that your statement is true, as a rule? Write down each general statement, and beneath it list all the details which support the statement. Try to use provable facts rather than opinions and propaganda as supporting details. Keep your list for reference.

Time order. Is your purpose to relate events as they actually took place? Separate the events according to when they happened, and then list them from first to last in the order of the passing of time (chronological order). You may have to do some checking to be sure your list is in time order.

Question/answer. Have you discovered the answer to certain general questions as the result of your research? Many reports are assigned for the purpose of answering a question rather than exploring a topic. Actually, the answers to research questions may cover a variety of topics. Answer each part of the general research question separately, and prepare to explain specific questions you can't answer.

Cause/effect. Do you intend to show what happened and why it happened? List the causes apart from their effects. Some effects may, in turn, cause other things to happen (as in a chain reaction). Be sure that you are sure of the order in which the events took place, as well as the reasons underlying each event.

Make a separate outline for each topic or pattern you decide to include in your report. If you have written summaries instead of taking notes, label each with the topic it discusses. Then use the topics to organize your research into outline form. Outlines help you organize a variety of information into one overall plan. The reader of your report will appreciate your efforts in making your presentation a logical one.

Graham and Robinson

The final arrangement of your outlines should be a complete plan for writing your report. If your information is incomplete, do further research to fill in what you're missing. Use your judgment to decide whether anything important has been overlooked. If nothing has been overlooked, you're ready for the last step in the report writing process.

Step 4.   Express Your Meaning As Best You Can

Plan to write a rough draft of your report. Don't expect to write the finished report in one sitting. A rough draft gives you the opportunity to get your ideas on paper without undue concern for spelling, punctuation, or grammar. Try to think in terms of paragraphs:
- a separate paragraph to introduce the main topic(s)
- a separate paragraph or two to develop each specific topic
- a separate paragraph to make a smooth change between topics
- a summary paragraph to review the important points you have made after each main topic and at the end of your report

If you find a paragraph particularly difficult to write, chances are that there may be some source of confusion for your reader. This may be a signal to include a reader aid (such as a map, table, illustration, diagram, or graph). Keep in mind that the sources of direct and indirect quotes will be of interest to your reader. If your teacher requires footnotes, follow the form you have been given. If not, let the reader know where you got your information. A list of sources used in the preparation of your report, called a bibliography, placed at the end is one good way to let your readers know where you got your information. A table of contents can help the reader anticipate your plan of organization, and should be included in longer reports. At this point your report should be almost complete—all it needs is a title.

Now show your rough draft to a friend or someone who will read it and ask questions that will help you make ideas clearer. Write your second draft with the intent of clarifying ideas; don't worry too much about spelling, punctuation, and sentence structure. Reread your second draft and have a friend read it to you. Clear up any meaning problems.

Now, your last job is to take your second draft and "polish" it. Proofread every sentence and correct your spelling, punctuation, and grammar. Write the final draft (or type it) as neatly and accurately as you can. Keep in mind that the reader cares about the appearance of your finished report. Businesses spend large sums of money on attractive packages for their products. To get the most from the time and energy you have invested in your report, make that final draft shine.

Games and Simulations

Unlike tests and reports, most students enjoy taking part in games and simulations related to study assignments. Test taking and report writing demand strategies for solving problems which are contrived by teachers primarily for the purposes of grading, and which are not necessarily related to real-life problem solving situations. The competition for grades is indirect, and a certain kind of temperment is required for consistent success. But not all great test-takers are great problem solvers. A different kind of competitive spirit is tapped during a game or simulation, where more active, dynamic problem solving strategies come into play. There is nothing wrong with educational fun and games, especially when they are linked directly to specific study goals and objectives.

Forms of creative expression other than creative writing serve as important checks on comprehension. For example, art work serves as an important comprehension check for students who have used much of their energy in the reading task, and for students who come to the English reading task from a bilingual background. Dramatics—plays and pantomimes—can provide readers with a vehicle for the expression of varied interpretations of what they've read. Pantomime, although limited as a communication medium, is useful to youngsters who come from a bilingual background as well as those youngsters who are hesitant to express themselves in other ways.

Computer simulation of real life situations is fast coming within reach of most teachers with the advent of the classroom microcomputer. Teachers with little or no programming experience can make use of educational simulations purchased in the marketplace. Students seem to enjoy solving the problems generated by computer programs, which demand a high level of individual interaction.

Using a Study Method

Effective study involves combining and balancing individual study strategies to complete a variety of tasks efficiently. Beyond the matter of individual learning styles, students differ in how well they manage their study strategies. Teachers may wish to suggest using a study method to students who have yet to discover effective and efficient ways of combining study strategies on their own. A study method is a general framework for helping students use their study skills and abilities productively. Several study methods have been suggested in the literature, each with its own mnemonic (SQ3R, OK4K, PQRST, etc.) to help students recall procedures to be employed before, during, and after reading for study purposes. Using a study method can be one of the last "crutches" students need before they're ready to go it alone.

The PQ5R Study Method

PQ5R is the mnemonic for an effective student regulated approach to studying the kind of material assigned every day—textbooks. Gaining new information and ideas from a variety of different textbooks demands a balanced and flexible network of study strategies. This method incorporates many of the teacher directed techniques previously discussed in this handbook into a student directed system that really works.

This explanation of PQ5R (From E.L. Thomas and H.A. Robinson, *Duplicator Masters for Improving Reading in Every Class.* Copyright © 1979 by Allyn and Bacon, Inc. Reprinted with permission.) is directed toward students in the secondary grades, although many primary grade students can make effective use of this information as well.

PQ5R—A Higher Level Approach to Studying a Textbook

For years psychologists have been experimenting to find out how students learn most easily. They have discovered shortcuts in study and have found ways to fix material firmly into the memory. The PQ5R approach to studying a textbook chapter packages *proven* study techniques into a smoothly operating system.

If you adopt just two or three of these techniques, you should upgrade the effectiveness of your study. If you adopt the whole package, you will have acquired the most powerful study procedure yet known for mastering a textbook chapter.

The steps in PQ5R are:

1. Preview   5. Recite
2. Question   6. Review
3. Read   7. Reflect   (There will be much overlapping
4. Record   of steps 2-7.)

P PREVIEW

Know where you're going first. You would never plunge in and try to cross rugged territory if you could have in advance an accurate map of the region. Here is your *mental map* of a textbook chapter. Examine the title. Read the introduction. "Hit the headings." Glance at the pictures, charts, and diagrams. Read the wrap-up of the chapter—the summary and review questions. Now you've taken the chill off the chapter.

Q QUESTION

Work through the chapter one manageable section at a time. A section marked off with a boldface or italic sideheading is likely to be the right size "bite" for you to digest.

Be a human question mark. Go into each section with a question in your mind. Turn headings, and sometimes topic sentences, into questions. These should guide you to the main points. Suppose a section has the boldface heading, **Solving the Population Problems Facing the World**. Quickly shift this into a question: "What are some possible solutions to the world's population problems?" Some boldface headings are quite general: **Human Population Growth**, for example. Then you might formulate the general question: "What are the important points made here about human population growth?" Use the authors' self-check questions. These are a giveaway of points the authors themselves consider important.

In actual experiments, college students who approached reading selections with questions showed decided gains in comprehension and better immediate and long term test performance.

You may find yourself reading effectively without this conscious questioning. In this case, just pick out the key ideas from the supporting material.

R1 READ

Read to find the answer to your question and other important content. Unknown terms say, STOP! LOOK UP! LEARN! Remove these roadblocks. Each pictorial aid is saying, "This is clearing up something important." Shift into back-and-forth reading for pictures, diagrams, and charts. Shift your eyes (and thoughts) back and forth as needed from the printed words to the pictorial aid.

Speed up and slow down as needed within the passage. Do stop-and-go reading. Thought time is needed in addition to reading time. Reread as often as necessary. Do "step-and-go" reading.

Graham and Robinson

R2   RECORD

Jot down or mark important ideas. Make the key ideas stand out in some way so they will "flag" you later. Use any combination of devices. Jot mininotes on a memo slip to be inserted between related pages or in the book's margin. Draw vertical lines in the margin just to the left or right of important content. Bracket key ideas. Underline or color-accent selectively. Now you won't have to reread the entire chapter when you return to review it later. Make key ideas "flag" you.

R3   RECITE

Students exclaim, "I've read that chapter twice, but I still can't remember it." Solve this problem by using the most powerful technique known to psychologists—the technique of self-recitation. As you complete a section or a paragraph, ask yourself, "Just what have I learned here?"

Look away from the book while you self-recite, or cover the passage with your hand or with a convenient card (such as 5" x 8" index card). Can you recite the important points to yourself in your own words? Now look back at the column of print, whenever you need to, and check your accuracy. Knowing you're going to self-recite when you finish a section forces you to concentrate while you're reading.

A Cover Card for Faster, Firmer Learning

You may find a cover card a convenient device.

Use it to conceal parts of your textbook (or notebook) as you recite important content you yourself—not by rote but with full appreciation of the meaning. Expose just the boldface heading and/or perhaps the first sentence of each paragraph while you see if you can recall what the section or paragraph contains. Then lift the card and check. Expose an "official" term, cover the definition, then try to explain the meaning. Cover an important diagram while you see if you've grasped its message and perhaps its parts and labels.

Experts in the psychology of learning advise you to "keep the print out of sight perhaps 50 percent of the time you are studying." They are suggesting that you look away from your book (or notes) in self-recitation, and thus change half-learned to more fully learned material.

Do you have trouble concentrating? Try a cover card. You can reread a passage and dream all the way through. The cover card forces you to concentrate as you struggle to recall what's underneath.

Self-recitation has been called the most powerful study technique known to psychologists.

Cover Card

Turn on triple strength learning. If you learn with your eyes alone, you're using just one-third of your sensory learning channels for mastering the printed page. Why not use all out VAK learning—VISUAL plus AUDITORY plus KINESTHETIC (muscular) learning? Use your eyes, then add your ears and your muscles. *See* it, *say* it, *hear* it, and *jot* it down. As you self-recite, you're changing half-learned to more fully learned material.

R4   REVIEW

Add a last quick run through. Can you recall the broad chapter plan? Run through the chapter to recall that plan. Next, run through it section by section, checking yourself once more on the main points and the important subpoints. Use your cover card again. Make some quick reviews later on from time to time. Long term memory does improve grades.

R5   REFLECT

As you read a passage, turn on your critical thinking. Ask yourself: "What does this all mean? Is it true? How can I apply it?" Reading and reflecting should be simultaneous and inseparable—built right into every step of PQ5R.

Are you locked into a rigid system in PQ5R? That is not intended. You'll want to vary any study system from one purpose to another, one textbook to another, one passage to another. Is PQ5R slow and labored? In a wartime crisis, an almost identical approach was used to rush young men through their training courses at Maxwell Air Base and other military locations.

You may want to try PQ5R as it is offered here, or you may want to modify it, or you may find it suggestive as you create your own study system to suit your own personal style.

The divided page technique (Thomas & Robinson, 1979, p.6). Some students can tell you why all the steps of PQ5R are important, yet won't actually see the method themselves. These students treat skills as content—they *know* but they don't *do*. You can help ensure that your students put theory into practice by showing them how to use the PQ5R method efficiently. The divided page technique is one convenient and practical way students can learn to organize PQ5R for regular use.

To make a divided page, students are instructed to fold a sheet of lined paper in half, forming two columns. On the left side of the page, the students turn headings, boldface print, words in italics, graphic aids, and other outward physical characteristics of the material into questions to be answered during the reading of the selection. The answers to the questions are written on the right side of the page. As each physical feature presents itself, a new question is asked and answered. This process continues until the entire selection has been read. Page numbers should be included in the margin beside each question for future reference. Questions left unanswered should be raised by the student in class. At this time, the teacher can provide 1) feedback about the quality of the students' question(s); 2) feedback about students' use of study strategies; and 3) specific answers to students' questions as necessary to ensure comprehension.

After the divided page has been completed, it may be used for study by folding the answers to keep them from view while students recite the answers to the questions. The divided page technique is effective because each step of the PQ5R study method is built in. It is practical because the only supplies needed are a sheet of note paper and a pen or pencil. Once students have mastered the technique they will find it can reduce their overall study time. The most important effect of using the technique is that it prepares students to direct their own learning activities. When our students are ready to teach themselves, our job is done.

Reaction Guide

I. Directions: Complete each statement with the correct word(s) from the list below.

1. Satisfying prereading purposes is called _____ _____.
2. Allow time after class discussion for _____ and _____ _____ of peers.
3. Organizing and storing information in memory involves _____, _____, _____, and _____.
4. Students should use the _____ and _____ to quiz themselves.
5. Students should take care to _____ _____ during a test.
6. Before a test, advise your students to read all choices and use the _____ _____ _____ when a guess is necessary.
7. Students can't write reports on their own until they have learned how to _____ primary and secondary sources, and _____ key information and ideas.
8. Students should _____ their notes into outline form before they _____ what they have learned in writing.

constructive criticism	buddy system	express
follow directions	application	self-recitation
locate	select	anticipatory comprehension
personalization	categorization	process of elimination
self-evaluation	organize	

II. Directions: Write each word from the word list above under the appropriate category.

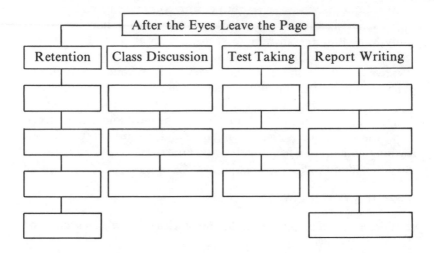

Reaction Guide Answers

I. Directions: Complete each statement with the correct word(s) from the list below.

1. Satisfying prereading purposes is called *anticipatory comprehension.*
2. Allow time after class discussion for *self-evaluation* and *constructive criticism* of peers.
3. Organizing and storing information in memory involves *personalization, application, categorization,* and *self-recitation.*
4. Students should use the *buddy system* to quiz themselves.
5. Students should take care to *follow directions* during a test.
6. Before a test, advise your students to read all choices and use the *process of elimination* when a guess is necessary.

Graham and Robinson

7. Students can't write reports on their own until they have learned how to *locate* primary and secondary sources, and *select* key information and ideas.
8. Students should *organize* their notes into outline form before they *express* what they have learned in writing.

constructive criticism   buddy system   express
follow directions   application   self-recitation
locate   select   anticipatory comprehension
personalization   categorization process of elimination
self-evaluation   organize

II. Directions: Write each word from the word list above under the appropriate category.

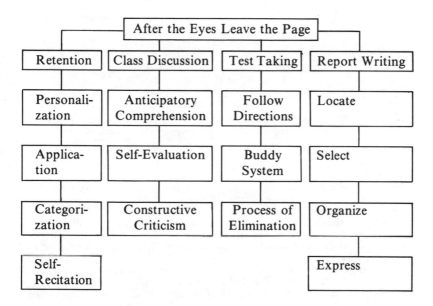

Divided Page Answers

Page Nos.	Questions	Answers
p. 97 100	What important purpose(s) can class discussion serve?	• Linking pre- and postorganizers • Helping students learn from each other
p. 100 101	How might students' retention strategies be improved?	*By making use of categorization, personalization, application, and self-recitation.*
p. 102 105	What five test taking strategies should teachers recommend to their students?	1. *Find out about and prepare for tests.* 2. *Give the test a once-over.* 3. *Budget your time.* 4. *Read directions and follow them.* 5. *Vary your approach as necessary.*
p. 107 113	What are four main steps in the report writing process?	1. *Locate your sources.* 2. *Select key information and ideas.* 3. *Organize according to your purposes.* 4. *Express meaning as best you can.*
p. 115 118	What does PQ5R stand for?	P. *preview* Q. *question* R. *read* R. *record* R. *recite* R. *review* R. *reflect*
p. 118	What is the purpose of the divided page technique?	*To ensure that the steps of the PQ5R are carried through effectively.*

References

American Optometric Association. *Teacher's guide to vision problems.* St. Louis, Missouri: American Optometric Association.

Anderson, T.H. Study strategies and adjunct aids. In R.J. Spiro, B.C. Bruce, & W.F. Brewer (Eds.), *Theoretical issues in reading comprehension.* Hillsdale, New Jersey: Erlbaum, 1980.

Ausubel, D.P. *Educational psychology: A cognitive view.* New York: Holt, Rinehart and Winston, 1968.

Blanc, S.S., Fischler, A.S., & Gardner, O. *Modern science: Earth, space, and environment.* New York: Holt, Rinehart and Winston, 1967.

Bond, G.L., Tinker, M.A., & Wasson, B.B. *Reading difficulties: Their diagnosis and correction* (4th ed.). Englewood Cliffs, New Jersey: Prentice-Hall, 1979.

Brandwein, P.F., & Others. *Matter: Its forms and changes.* New York: Harcourt Brace Jovanovich, 1972.

Brandwein, P.F., & Others. *Life: A biological science.* New York: Harcourt Brace Jovanovich, 1975.

Brown, A.L. Metacognitive development and reading. In R.J. Spiro, B.C. Bruce, & W.F. Brewer (Eds.), *Theoretical issues in reading comprehension.* Hillsdale, New Jersey: Erlbaum, 1980.

Clymer, T., & Others. *To turn a stone.* Boston: Ginn, 1970.

Graham and Robinson

Dale, E. *Audiovisual methods in teaching* (3rd ed.). New York: Holt, Rinehart and Winston, 1969.

Dempsey, J.H. *Let freedom ring: A history of the United States* (teacher's ed.). Morristown, New Jersey: Silver Burdett, 1980.

Earle, R.A. Reading and mathematics: Research in the classroom. In H.A. Robinson & E.L. Thomas (Eds.), *Fusing reading skills and content.* Newark, Delaware: International Reading Association, 1969.

Early, M., & Others. *Expanding horizons.* New York: Harcourt Brace Jovanovich, 1979.

Edison, M., & Heimann, S.F. *Public opinion polls.* New York: Franklin Watts, 1972.

Estes, T.H., & Vaughan, J.L., Jr. *Reading and learning in the content classroom.* Boston: Allyn and Bacon, 1978.

Feirer, J.L., & Lindbeck, J.R. *Basic metalwork.* Peoria, Illinois: Charles A. Bennett, 1978.

Fodor, J.T., & Others. *A healthier you.* River Forest, Illinois: Laidlaw Brothers, 1980.

Goodman, K.S. Reading: A psycholinguistic guessing game. In H. Singer & R.B. Ruddell (Eds.), *Theoretical models and processes of reading* (2nd ed.). Newark, Delaware: International Reading Association, 1976.

Gough, P.B. One second of reading. In H. Singer & R.B. Ruddell (Eds.), *Theoretical models and processes of reading* (2nd ed.). Newark, Delaware: International Reading Association, 1976.

Halsey, W.D. (Ed.). *Collier's encyclopedia.* New York: Macmillan, 1974.

Hammond world atlas. Maplewood, New Jersey: Hammond, Inc., 1971.

Herber, H.L. *Teaching reading in content areas.* Englewood Cliffs, New Jersey: Prentice-Hall, 1978.

Langer, J.A. From theory to practice: A prereading plan. *Journal of Reading*, 1981, *25*, 152-156.

Manzo, A.V. The ReQuest procedure. *Journal of Reading*, 1969, *13*, 123-126, 163.

Miller, W.H. *Reading diagnosis kit.* New York: Center for Applied Research in Education, 1978.

Readers' guide to periodical literature, 1982, *82*, 119.

Roget's international thesaurus (4th ed.). New York: Harper & Row, 1977.

Robinson, H.A. *Teaching reading, writing, and study strategies: The content areas.* Boston: Allyn and Bacon, 1983.

Robinson, H.A., & Hall, M. *Content area reading skills: Reference, level e.* Concord, California: EDL, A Division of Arista Corporation, 1980.

Robinson, H.A., & Hall, M. *Content area reading skills: Reference, level f.* Concord, California: EDL, A Division of Arista Corporation, 1980.

Robinson, H.A., & Hollander, S.K. *Content area reading skills: Social studies, level GHI.* Concord, California: EDL, A Division of Arista Corporation, 1980.

Rumelhart, D.E. Toward an interactive model of reading. In S. Dornic (Ed.), *Attention and performance VI.* Hillsdale, New Jersey: Erlbaum, 1977.

Safir, F. *Adventures in reading* (heritage ed.). New York: Harcourt Brace Jovanovich, 1980.

Schwartz, S., & O'Connor, J.R. *Exploring our nation's history, volume 2: The age of greatness since the Civil War.* New York: Globe Book, 1971.

Smith, F. *Understanding reading.* New York: Holt, Rinehart and Winston, 1971.

Smith, N.B. *Be a better reader, book I.* Englewood Cliffs, New Jersey: Prentice-Hall, 1963.

Thomas, E.L., & Robinson, H.A. *Duplicator masters for improving reading in every class.* Boston: Allyn and Bacon, 1979.

Thomas, E.L., & Robinson, H.A. *Improving reading in every class* (3rd ed.). Boston: Allyn and Bacon, 1982.

Thorndike, E.L., & Barnhart, C.L. *Thorndike Barnhart advanced dictionary.* Glenview, Illinois: Scott, Foresman, 1974.

Twain, M. The cat and the pain killer. In E.C. O'Daly & E.W. Neiman, *Adventures for readers, book one.* New York: Harcourt Brace Jovanovich, 1963.

Webster's third new international dictionary of the English language: Unabridged. Springfield, Massachusetts: G. & L. Merriam, 1976.

Wildman, D.H., & Kling, M. Semantic, syntactic, and spatial anticipation in reading. *Reading Research Quarterly,* 1978-1979, No. 2, 160.

World almanac and book of facts 1982. New York: Newspaper Enterprise Association, 1982.